HOW TO DO
GREAT WORK
WITHOUT BEING
AN ASSHOLE

by PAUL WOODS

LAURENCE KING PUBLISHING

Published in 2019 by
Laurence King Publishing Ltd
361-373 City Road
London EC1V 1LR
Tel +44 20 7841 6900
Fax +44 20 7841 6910
enquiries@laurenceking.com
www.laurenceking.com

ISBN 978 1 78627 391 8

Commissioning editor: Sophie Drysdale
Senior editor: Gaynor Sermon
Design: TurnbullGrey

Printed in China

CONTENTS

FOREWORD

YOU CAN'T UNLEARN
TO BE AN ASSHOLE

Paul asked me to write a few words for this book. We obviously like each other or he wouldn't have asked and I wouldn't have written. So we're past the asshole barrier already.

Over the past 50 years or so (yes, I am that old), I've worked with hundreds of colleagues, having hired most of them myself. I didn't know it in the beginning, and if I had I probably wouldn't have admitted it: I've always hired people because I liked them, asking myself, "Do I want to spend 8-10 hours a day with this person in the same room? And would the rest of the team think likewise?" Most designers can pick up specific skills in a few weeks, learn proper typography (ok, that'll take years), write clean code, make very good espresso. But you can never unlearn to be an asshole.

The best people I've hired came from the weirdest backgrounds—carpenters, chefs, soldiers, historians—not the usual smooth ride through academia for them. A willingness to learn, to fit in, and to give their best is more important than having passed exams. Do not rely on portfolios (I've seen too many with copies of other people's work—digital makes that easy), trust your gut.

Employees move on. They become competitors, peers, often enough clients. And they'll remember how you treated them back then. It always hurts when someone leaves, especially when they started as beginners and you taught them a few of their first tricks. But they need to move, or else they think that your way of doing things is the only way. It certainly is not. But they'll stay in touch and will treat you as a friend later on if you treated them decently back then. When Paul left Edenspiekermann Berlin after a few years there, I was disappointed. At the same time I knew that he had to in order to learn and get better. We kept in touch and: Bingo! Years later, we work together again.

The German proverb says: As you shout into the woods, it will shout back at you (*Wie man in den Wald hineinruft, so schallt es zurück*). Lousy translation, but you get the gist.

I rest my case. At any rate, you have a whole book in front of you with Paul making his case, which happens to be our case.

Dr. h.c. Erik Spiekermann

PREFACE

A framed poster hangs on the wall near the front entrance to the office of our downtown Los Angeles agency. Printed on a 1961 Korrex Frankfurt Kraft press, it is probably the most popular piece of wall decoration I have ever come across. Almost every person who visits the agency—from Hollywood celebrities to investment bankers—comments on the poster, often taking a selfie in front of it so that their colleagues, friends, or fans associate them with its message. Designed by type designer and entrepreneur Erik Spiekermann, the poster simply reads: "Don't work for assholes. Don't work with assholes."

If not working for assholes is so ubiquitously cherished by all manner of people, why is it that so many of us do? In the creative industries, "The Asshole" and the toxic culture that follows them is found more often than a nun in a nunnery.

Over the years, I've had many friends who work for CEOs, creative directors, account directors, and who-the-hell-cares directors who are not just assholes, but assholes who pride themselves on being assholes. It could be the ego-driven creative director who imparts his off-the-cuff whims and last-minute feedback to designers at 5.50pm on a Friday before a Monday morning client presentation; an HR department that doesn't reply to unsuccessful job applications; or a CEO who fosters a work environment where staff feel the need to regularly work long hours under the guise of "living the dream." The creative industries have long had a reputation of being filled with people who would be more at home running a prison camp than mentoring impressionable young talent in an agency environment.

However, things are showing signs of changing, albeit slowly. In the past, young talent simply had to endure the long hours, the egomaniacs, and all manner of other unfavorable working practices due to the lack of alternative career paths where they could scratch their creative itch in exchange for a steady paycheck. But nowadays, with the vast array of viable alternatives, including tech companies, startups, and expanding in-house design teams, the best talent can pick and choose their career options with no need to involve bad culture and egos.

Despite the signs of a positive shift in attitudes, old habits die hard. Unsustainable work practices are still commonplace in creative agencies, and these result in burnout, high staff turnover, and poor-quality work. When you work in a toxic environment, neither the individual, the client, nor the work itself benefits.

This book explores the simple question: "Can you do great work without being an asshole?"

Is this a naive undertaking in an industry not known either for sustainable work practices or being free of egos? Can it be done in a way that maintains a competitive advantage, keeps your clients happy, and, perhaps most crucially, still produces great work?

As you work through this book, you'll notice recurring comparisons between my time working in Germany and my time in the USA. The cultural difference between creative agencies in Northern European (Germany, Sweden, Denmark, etc.) and Western English-speaking nations (USA, UK, Ireland, etc.) is huge. Northern Europeans put a big focus on efficient work practices, whereas the latter tend to put the work above all else, regardless of the implications on personal life. Having worked in both cultures, I can see there are definite merits to both working styles. This book attempts to compare the best (and worst) features of both.

Yours sincerely,

Paul Woods

P.S. You're probably thinking "the person writing this seems like a bit of an asshole themselves." This statement is possibly not entirely untrue.

BEING NICE
IS GOOD BUSINESS

Traditionally in the creative industries, the work has always come first; being an asshole was entirely acceptable once you had picked up a few awards along the way. While that's all well and good in the short term, internal culture all too often gets left behind in the rush to produce great work.

Great agency culture matters. If you want to do great work, it matters. If you want to attract the best staff, it matters. If you want to build client relationships, it matters. And even if you are a truly soulless creature who cares only about a quick buck, it still matters. Although creative agencies have never had a problem with producing great work, they have had a more troubled past with regard to maintaining positive work environments and treating staff well. Now, in the information age where there are no secrets, these chickens are finally coming home to roost.

BAD CULTURE IN THE CREATIVE INDUSTRIES

Anyone who has worked in the creative industries in London, New York, or almost any other major city, will probably agree that bad culture, egos, and ludicrous working hours are not only common but are often celebrated. Interns are not paid. Long hours are worn as a badge of pride. Egomania is encouraged, and it is generally understood that the larger the ego, the more revered and "legendary" the individual is.

Like most people who have worked in the creative industries, I have encountered many individuals who embody the very worst industry stereotypes. Over the course of this book, you will be introduced to some of the most colorful ones that I have come across. The first such character I will share with you is especially memorable. This fine gentleman—let's call him Denny Dribblehoff—was a particularly bad apple.

GREAT AGENCY CULTURE MATTERS. IF YOU WANT TO DO GREAT WORK, IT MATTERS. IF YOU WANT TO ATTRACT THE BEST STAFF, IT MATTERS.

Denny was not a Steve Jobs-esque creative genius, but an account director managing a large corporate client. Account directors like this embody the very worst traits of the creative industries. Admittedly, they have one of the toughest jobs in the industry, juggling unreasonable client demands with realistic timelines for producing the actual creative work. Over the years, I have worked with some wonderful account directors who understood what it takes to make great work; Denny Dribblehoff was not one them. Denny was from an obscure town called something like Ballsberg or Shitsville. Relatively new to city life, he was placed in charge of managing a large—and rather tricky—corporate client. He walked with the swagger of a fooball player, dressed in an ill-fitting black suit and tie which gave the impression that he was permanently on his way to a funeral, and on the rare occasion when he let his hair down, he could not handle his drink. He was a nightmare to every creative team at the agency. Without fail, around 5pm on almost any given Friday before a deadline, Denny would come by the design department and in his thickest Midwestern accent say: "All right guys. The client loooooooves the creative. Great ... genius stuff—never seen anything like it. Those words, right out of her mouth. There's a Webby Award on the way for this one! Now, we have a few changes to make ...."

Denny would then rattle off a long list of changes that amounted to coming up with a totally new idea over the weekend and finishing it before

THE BAD HABITS OF
THE CREATIVE INDUSTRIES

LONG HOURS

EGOS

POOR TREATMENT
OF JUNIORS

CHAOTIC
WORKFLOWS

the 9am deadline on Monday morning. He would then inform us he had an important family event to attend and had to leave right away, but would see us all on Monday, "... bright and early, guys!" and leave the office with a spring in his step.

While common sense in that situation would be for the design team to tell Denny to go to hell before bludgeoning him to a bloody pulp with his patent-leather shoes, such is the conditioning in creative agencies that creatives see this type of request as a challenge: "Are you good enough to produce an award-winning piece of work in three days? Dilly and Johnny won a big pitch by working over the course of a single weekend and now there's talk of them winning a Cannes Gold Lion."

Account directors like Denny understand the creative disposition all too well, and know exactly how and when to push the ego and insecurity buttons of creatives. It is no wonder that many older creatives I know working in agencies are divorced. In the creative industries, your personal life can go screw itself. By the way, Denny is still alive and working at the same agency; he hasn't (yet) been bludgeoned with his own shoes, or anything else for that matter.

THE DRIVE FOR EXCELLENCE AT ALL COSTS

Creative directors are some of the worst offenders when it comes to cultivating bad work environments. Conditioned by years of long hours, weekend work, and egos as juniors themselves, they have come to accept that personal life has no place in the creative industries, and now will do everything in their power to produce a "great" piece of work. It's a vicious cycle. After someone has spent a few years in the creative industries, the focus on producing excellence every single time becomes a blinding force regardless of the assignment.

DISCERN THE PROJECTS THAT ARE WORTH SACRIFICING PERSONAL TIME FOR FROM THE CRAP THAT BENEFITS NO ONE

This striving for excellence blinds you from discerning the projects that are worth sacrificing personal time for from the crap that benefits no one. I've worked like a maniac on some worthwhile projects that deserved my personal time, such as working 20-hour days on-site in South Africa designing a platform that promotes social entrepreneurs in poorer communities. This project mattered. However—especially earlier in my career—I also sacrificed many, many, many hours of my personal life on projects that were of no value to anyone, least of all me. In fact, nobody outside our team's circle of creative insanity would ever care about the work we were creating. Remember the banner ad campaign that you worked on for 15 hours a day and missed two weekends for? Only 0.05% of people[1] who see it will ever click on it. It is trash. Nobody needs it. Nobody cares.

A well-known advertising agency sports the slogan "The Work. The Work. The Work." This mantra perfectly sums up the intense culture of pressure that agencies foster wherein people are expected to go to any lengths to produce excellence for just about any assignment. When you take a step back from this, you realize this behavior is insane. Reality check: You are helping corporations to sell cheap phone packages, fizzy drinks, chocolate bars, and all manner of other useless products. Is this worth sacrificing your personal life, your family, and your friends for? Unfortunately, for many years in the creative industries, the answer was a resounding yes.

WHAT HAS CHANGED?

The question is, why is not being an asshole suddenly so important? After all, the creative industries have been around for decades, making billions of dollars a year, and picking up countless awards along the way, regardless of their toxic work practices. Why change now? The reason is very simple: At the heart of great creative work are great people. Unsurprisingly, great people will only stay in your agency if they are happy and, in the digital age, the best talent is empowered with more choice and information than ever before.

GREAT PEOPLE WILL ONLY STAY IN YOUR AGENCY IF THEY ARE HAPPY

[1] https://www.smartinsights.com/internet-advertising/internet-advertising-analytics/display-advertising-clickthrough-rates/

GOOD CULTURE

Almost 6pm— time for the team to go home

We need a proper briefing for the new project

The full team will present to the client

We actually reply to job applications

We credit the whole team in award applications

All interns will be paid fairly

BAD CULTURE

STIFF COMPETITION FROM TECH COMPANIES

In recent years, the agency model, once the only game in town, has begun to lose its exclusivity, as the best people are increasingly being lured away by more appealing and more lucrative offers from the deep pockets in Silicon Valley. Tech companies such as Google, Facebook, and others often offer more competitive salaries, flexible working hours, and a plethora of other perks that agencies find it hard to compete with.

In addition to the salary and benefits, the excitement of being part of an actual product or a startup is tremendously appealing to young talent. A couple of years ago, I was offered a job at a big tech firm in San Francisco and, despite being an "agency guy" through and through, I was tempted. I even took part in a round of interviews with the firm, and I was very pleasantly surprised at what they had to offer creatives. Had I not recently moved my family from Europe to New York, I would not have hesitated to leave the agency world behind.

CLIENT-SIDE IS MORE POPULAR THAN EVER

In-house teams at non-tech companies are growing too. While I was working agency-side in New York, I saw quite a few people leave for in-house roles at traditionally "non-creative" companies. And it is no wonder: When it comes to digital products, client-side is a very attractive place to be. Creatives get to work on projects with more focus on getting the details right, rather than rushing from project to project, and often get to work in a more sustainable environment.

THE GUILTY ARE NAMED AND SHAMED

Although the creative industries have always had a less-than-stellar reputation when it came to working practices, in the past, given the allure, young talent were happy to go along with the toxic culture in the name of forwarding their careers. However, there are no secrets in the digital age and talent can easily discern what roles and clients have good or bad cultures. Sites such as Glassdoor mean that staff can speak their minds anonymously and their reviews are publicly available to potential hires and potential clients. It only takes a quick search to find evidence of bad culture, once hidden behind closed doors, laid bare for all to see.

CREATIVE PROJECTS ARE MORE LONG-TERM THAN EVER

As marketing budgets are increasingly poured into digital projects, the industry needs to shift toward a longer-term model and away from the traditional "churn and burn." Unlike the process of creating a TV spot or a marketing campaign, building a digital product is a slow process, taking months or years rather than weeks. These types of long-term projects require an entirely different mindset from the fast and furious approach typically employed by traditional agencies.

BEING NICE IS GOOD BUSINESS

Let's be very clear about something. Producing great work means working fucking hard—there is no shortcut. It does not mean checking out at 5pm. It does not mean sitting on Facebook during the day or taking leisurely two-hour lunch breaks. It does mean occasionally working late nights to push something from being good to being great. It might mean working an odd weekend before the final deadline of a long project. But long hours, inefficiency, and bad culture should be the exception, not the rule. It is not an excuse for a lack of respect for people's personal lives. It is not an excuse for having an ego the size of a planet.

PRODUCING GREAT WORK MEANS WORKING FUCKING HARD—THERE IS NO SHORTCUT.

First and foremost, you work in the creative industries. You are not an artist. It is a commercial occupation. It is a fun occupation for sure, and a very meaningful one, but it is not something to sacrifice your life for.

In my career, I have been very lucky to have worked at some great companies with fantastic internal culture that still consistently produce great work. Believe me, it's a tough balance to get right and it requires a lot of effort on all sides. However, building a great culture is simply no longer an optional "nice to have." Simply put, if you are an asshole, your best people will leave. When the best people leave, the work suffers. And when this happens, the clients will not be far behind.

AM I AN ASSHOLE?

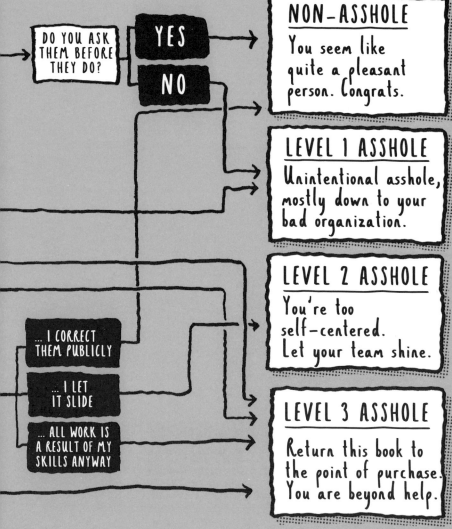

JUNIOR   MID-LEVEL

SENIOR   EXECUTIVE

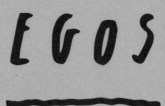

EGOS

With rare exceptions, the creative individual falls into one of two categories: The deeply insecure, or the egomaniac. The former lives in a state of constant self-doubt and is in need of continuous validation. In fact, they are usually the best people in an agency, as they are constantly pushing themselves to improve. Unfortunately, their need for validation means that they are easily manipulated and taken advantage of by the latter group, the egomaniacs — the subject of this chapter.

Perhaps there is a deep unconscious connection between these two types of individual. However, lacking any training in matters of the mind, I can simply say this: Egos have no place in the creative industries. Removing these types of behaviors, and if necessary these types of people, will result in a better work environment for everybody, more autonomous and profitable teams, and — most importantly — better work.

UNDERSTANDING THE EGOMANIAC

To understand why egos have no place in the creative industries, let's take a more detailed look at the egomaniac. These individuals are usually (although not always) part of the creative department and are most often senior in title. They have a deep-rooted belief that they are the source of all greatness at the agency lucky enough to be graced with their presence. They see themselves as a sort of modern-day messiah, and their opinion is always right. All ideas for a project must come from them, and the ideas of others are rarely considered—unless they can take credit for them. They show a flagrant lack of respect for people's time. In short, they believe that others exist only to build their personal reputation.

Creative directors usually win the top spot on the agency's egomaniac list. To be fair, perhaps this is not entirely their fault. At large agencies, creative directors are placed on a pedestal by the lowly account teams and presented as a sort of mystical Christ-like figure to clients. To some extent, this sort of treatment would rub off on anyone. However, while it's all well and good to play the Mystical Christ to clients, it's a whole other situation to act like this around your team.

IT'S ALL WELL AND GOOD TO PLAY THE MYSTICAL CHRIST TO CLIENTS, IT'S A WHOLE OTHER SITUATION TO ACT LIKE THIS AROUND YOUR TEAM

One of the most memorable Mystical Christs I've encountered was an old-school creative director—let's call him Willy Wunderwinkle—whose favorite pastime was to take on projects with impossible deadlines on behalf of his team. Willy would bounce enthusiastically into the project room to brief our team on the "exciting new pitch," resulting in a collective internal groan, as we knew that the next few days would result in little or no sleep. Willy would then vanish for the next five days. He couldn't be found at his desk, in any conference room, or indeed anywhere in the agency. He wouldn't answer emails or text messages from our team requesting his feedback, which increasingly grew more frequent and desperate as the deadline loomed closer. Then, on the day of the deadline, Willy would reappear in the agency in a resurrection fashion worthy of a true Mystical Christ. In a blasé tone, Willy would inform our team that, unbeknown to us, he had briefed a second team to work on the same brief and he would be presenting their work today and not ours.

Like many other characters in this book, Willy is still alive and was never fired—or, for that matter, murdered by the team of junior designers working under him. In fact, I'm fairly certain he's been promoted a couple of times since we last met.

EGOMANIAC TYPES

THE HOVERING
ART DIRECTOR

"I'M TOO GOOD FOR
DEADLINES" DESIGNER

CREDIT-TAKING
CREATIVE DIRECTOR

THE OBLIVIOUSLY
LOUD ACCOUNT GUY

"I'M-A-DESIGNER"
CLIENT

"I'M-TOO-IMPORTANT-
TO-SHOW-UP" CEO

THOUGHTS OF AN EGOMANIAC

EGOMANIACS ARE BAD FOR BUSINESS

Dear creative directors, and indeed everyone else: Leave your egos at home or on the conference hall stage. There is simply no reason for egomaniacs to exist in the creative workplace. Egos stifle team growth, negatively affect the quality of the work, and cost an agency money.

EGOS STIFLE THE GROWTH OF INDIVIDUALS AND TEAMS

One of the worst aspects of the egomaniac personality is their lack of trust in others. They need to micromanage every piece of work that goes out the door and cannot delegate successfully. They truly believe that they, and only they, can do this task correctly. I've had senior creative directors on large salaries insist on reviewing every single resize of a banner campaign by a production designer. Although I believe that attention to detail is critical, this is fucking insanity. This level of micromanaging means that a team can never make its own decisions or grow as individuals.

EGOS COST AN AGENCY MONEY

By consistently acting as a bottleneck in the creative process, egomaniacs screw project budgets and timelines by not providing timely feedback and ignoring the realities of production timelines. They are of the opinion that achieving their personal "artistic vision" is more important than the overall success of a project from a feasibility and financial perspective.

EGOMANIACS SCREW PROJECT BUDGETS AND TIMELINES

EGOS DRIVE YOUR BEST PEOPLE AWAY

An egomaniac will rarely share the spotlight with anyone else. They take the best assignments for themselves and leave the least interesting assignments to everyone else. They rarely mentor young talent as they are too intent on achieving their creative vision. Talented young creatives will only tolerate this for so long before they leave for somewhere where they have the opportunity to shine.

CREATING AN EGO-FREE CULTURE

Want to create an ego-free workplace? It is not easy. The creative industries are riddled with mentally disturbed hotheads, self-doubters, insomniacs, and a whole host of other eccentric personality types that are rarely logical or reasonable. However, keep in mind that creative workplaces are commercial operations. You are not an artist; you are a professional who can and should be capable of behaving like an adult. Here are the two most important things that anyone in a creative leadership position can do to reduce the levels of egomania in the creative workplace.

LET YOUR PEOPLE DO THEIR DAMN JOBS

Stop micromanaging. Trust your team and allow them do their jobs. If you have a valid reason to not trust your team, fire them. As former Apple CEO Steve Jobs once famously said: "It doesn't make sense to hire smart people and tell them what to do; we hire smart people so they can tell *us* what to do." An egomaniac never trusts their team and always needs to make the final decision themselves. In a 2007 interview[2], Donald J. Trump stated that he doesn't believe in hiring people who are smarter than himself. If that doesn't convince you to let your people do their job, then I honestly don't know what will.

ALWAYS GIVE CREDIT WHERE CREDIT IS DUE

Never take credit for work you didn't do. Once again, creative directors are often the worst offenders here, especially when it comes to presenting work to others. Always give credit where credit is due. Be humble and correct people when the efforts of others are wrongly attributed to you. If you are in a senior role, you should always deflect personal praise from clients away from you and insist that it is directed to your team. As someone in a senior role, you don't need the platitudes—your job is to grow your team, not your ego. When I was a junior designer, I worked with a creative director who made a point of highlighting team efforts at every opportunity. When presenting work to a client, he would always include a team slide listing everyone—from intern to senior—who worked on the project. As a junior, a role that rarely sees recognition from clients, this meant the world to me.

YOUR JOB IS TO GROW YOUR TEAM, NOT YOUR EGO.

[2] http://www.cnbc.com/2016/12/19/donald-trump-hiring-people-smarter-than-you-is-a-mistake.html

WHEN YOU DO NEED EGOS

Don't get me wrong: Individuals with larger-than-life personalities play a critical role in acting as an internal role model, external brand-building, and defining the voice of a creative agency. The biggest names in design and advertising—Stefan Sagmeister, Erik Spiekermann, and Bob Greenberg, to name a few—have built their businesses around their large, public personalities, backed up, of course, by great work. Having a loud, outspoken personality gives an agency a public face and a voice that promotes and defines its brand. But while these public personas can be loud, controversial, and sometimes even offensive, they are just that—public personas. Having a big personality in public is very different to having an ego with your team in day-to-day work.

HAVING A BIG PERSONALITY IN PUBLIC IS VERY DIFFERENT TO HAVING AN EGO WITH YOUR TEAM

I worked with Erik Spiekermann for several years in Berlin. He is a larger-than-life personality, always the loudest voice in the room, the most outspoken in interviews or at conferences. He is never afraid to express controversial opinions. But, when back at his agency with his team, he is one of the most respectful and encouraging creative directors I've worked with. In particular, he pays close attention to junior staff, always knowing their names and consistently encouraging them. He gives credit where credit is due, publicly correcting others when he is incorrectly credited with something that someone else did. If one of the biggest names in design can do this successfully for more than 40 years, surely your ego can take a back seat too?

MEETINGS

When it comes to the subject of meetings, I will let you in on a little secret: Only assholes like useless meetings. Every normal human being hates them. In my experience, the vast majority of creative or project-related meetings are unnecessary.

Unnecessary meetings waste time, and the respective topic could often be handled much more effectively over a quick IM or in-person chat. They rack up client budgets that could be better spent on producing the work itself. Badly prepared meetings are even worse. A meeting without a clear purpose and concrete next steps will sow confusion and send creatives on a wild goose chase for days. In short, any project, agency, or team will run more efficiently and ultimately produce better work if meetings are minimal in quantity, as short as possible, and always laser-focused in purpose. When it comes to meetings, think like a German, and you won't go too far wrong.

ASSHOLES AND MEETINGS

The egomaniac loves meetings of all kinds. The more useless the meeting, the better! A meeting has a ready-made audience to listen to them talk. They can stand up at the top of the room and look important. They can draw silly squiggly lines on a whiteboard and then point to them. They can pretend to listen to the ideas of others before interrupting with their own groundbreaking epiphany. For the egomaniac, a useless meeting is like Christmas morning for a six-year-old.

FOR THE EGOMANIAC A USELESS MEETING IS LIKE CHRISTMAS MORNING FOR A SIX-YEAR-OLD.

During my years working in creative agencies, I've met many individuals who loved useless meetings. One who stands out—let's call him Cyril Crumplehorn—was a project manager in his late twenties with an incredibly annoying voice. When I first met him, he was running a relatively unimportant B-list project, which, unfortunately, I was also working on. Cyril was a tremendously self-centered character. His presence in any room was like a hurricane; he was not happy until he had disturbed just about everyone within a ten-mile radius. He was the sort of person about whom comedy sitcoms like *The Office* are made. Above all, Cyril loved the sound of his own voice.

Cyril gained great pleasure in hosting lengthy meetings with the full team, often lasting over two hours, with little purpose other than having a vague title such as "Update," or "Project Status." During a particularly time-intensive project, Cyril increased the frequency of these meetings to twice a day: "Morning Update" and "Afternoon Update." Attendance at both meetings was mandatory for the entire team to update Cyril on what had been done since the last update meeting two hours previously. Invariably, Cyril would use the meeting as a soapbox to share his opinions on everything from why he didn't like the choice of font color to what he thought of the latest episode of *Keeping Up With the Kardashians*.

Cyril would always involve the maximum number of people possible in every meeting. After all, why bother hosting a meeting if there was no audience to enjoy it? Not only would the project team be invited, he would also invite individuals from unrelated projects, miscellaneous staff, and management. Hell, even bring your kids. Invariably, regardless of the number of people attending or the amount of time in the room, everyone would leave the meeting asking themselves, "What just happened?"

One afternoon, Cyril held a particularly intensive meeting lasting over two hours. So intent was he on the meeting, that he failed to notice that, one by one, the entire project team had left the room. The only person remaining was his intern, listening earnestly to his every word. I have worked with many

Cyril-type characters since then but, for me, he was the original and I will always have a soft spot for his hilarious egomania.

It's not just assholes and egomaniacs who love meetings; there's cultural difference at play too. For example, Americans like meetings much more than Northern Europeans. They love discussing things in groups, brainstorming, and coming up with new ideas together. Germans, on the other hand, do not think much of this practice; instead, efficiency is often valued above all else.

The problem with excessive or inefficient meetings in our industry is that creative people are often easily distracted. We love to discuss, noodle, brainstorm, and then discuss some more. We seek validation from others. Put a group of creatives together with a disorganized meeting structure and, rest assured, nothing will get done. And when nothing gets done because of useless meetings, people have to work longer hours to get their actual shit done.

I worked with a German business partner for a number of years running a creative agency. He was a master of efficiency, and it was mostly because of his dedication to smart work practice that staff could leave on time every day. His pet peeve was useless meetings. I saw him grill people time and time again when they set up spontaneous, unprepared meetings that wasted everyone's time. Trust me, you don't want to piss off a German.

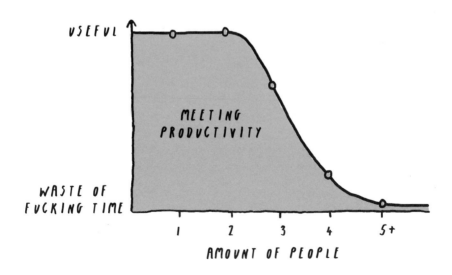

DO I EVEN NEED A MEETING?

Before you reach for the Calendar app, ask yourself: "Do I really need a meeting for this?" Would an email or a quick IM suffice? Or a quick one-on-one chat at the creative director's desk to discuss a client's feedback?

When it comes to creative work, there are only two occasions when in-person meetings are always necessary (or at least preferred). The first is project briefings. No project, large or small, should kick off without a well-prepared, in-person briefing with the full team where questions can be answered. All too often, creative projects begin with little or no briefing other than a short note via email like, "Create a new marketing page for the client like the one we did last month." There is no substitute for a clear, in-person briefing to produce work that meets the client's and the users' needs. (More on the subject of briefing later.)

The second occasion when in-person meetings are highly beneficial is presenting work. No matter how long or successful your relationship with a client, when it comes to presenting creative or design work, an in-person meeting is by far the best way to share the thinking behind it and to answer their questions or concerns. In my experience, a piece of work or an idea probably has double the chance of being sold through if it is presented to a client in person.

HOW TO RUN A PRODUCTIVE MEETING

Here are some things I learned from my uber-efficient business partner about running meetings "the German way." To give these points some context, let's use a real-world example: You've suddenly received some unsettling feedback about a logo design that your team is working on for "Brand XXX," a new product from the well-known adult toy manufacturer, "Company XXX." You need to call an urgent meeting to discuss how to proceed with your creative team. On the following pages you'll find three steps to ensure a productive and efficient meeting.

SHOULD I HOLD A MEETING?

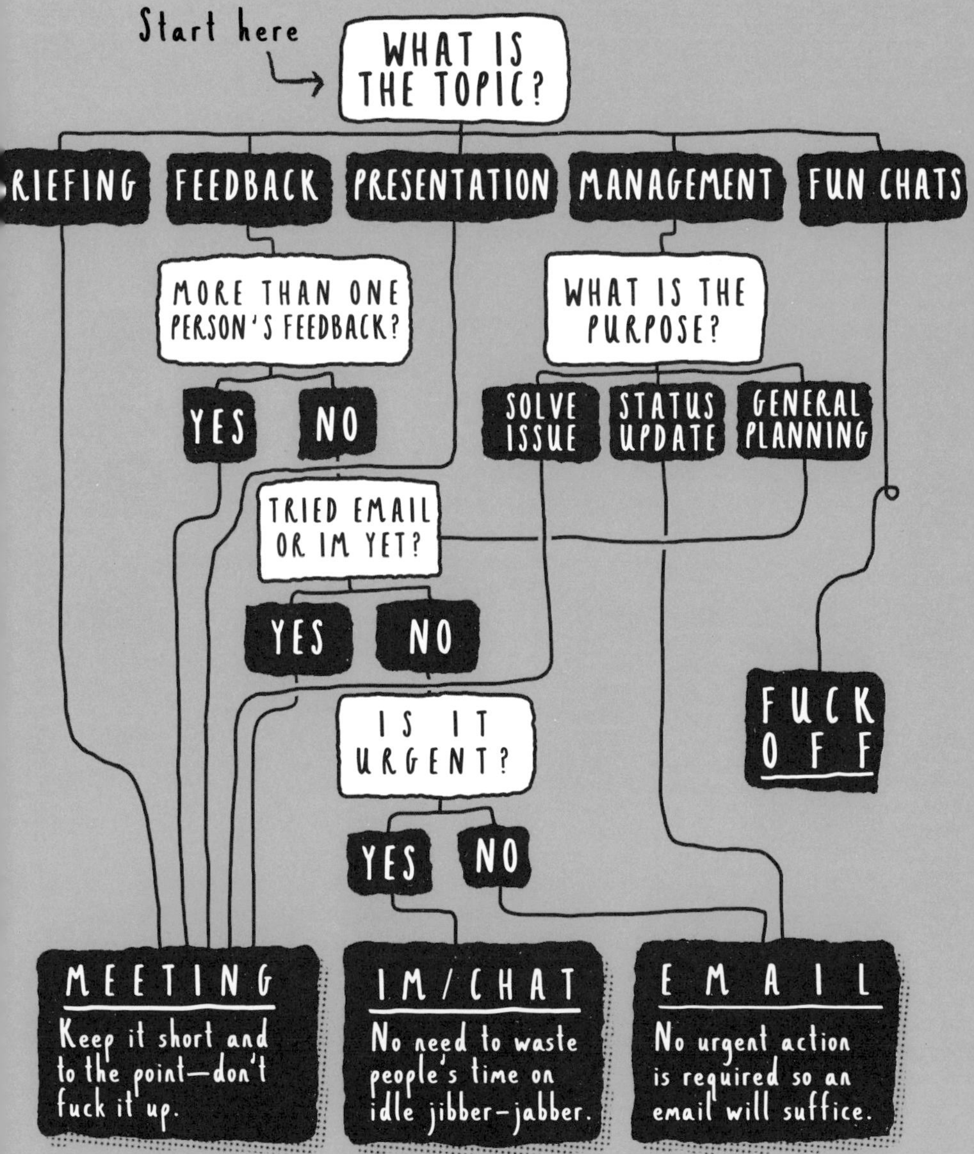

Start here →

WHAT IS THE TOPIC?

- BRIEFING
- FEEDBACK
- PRESENTATION
- MANAGEMENT
- FUN CHATS

MORE THAN ONE PERSON'S FEEDBACK?
- YES
- NO

WHAT IS THE PURPOSE?
- SOLVE ISSUE
- STATUS UPDATE
- GENERAL PLANNING

TRIED EMAIL OR IM YET?
- YES
- NO

IS IT URGENT?
- YES
- NO

FUCK OFF

MEETING
Keep it short and to the point—don't fuck it up.

IM/CHAT
No need to waste people's time on idle jibber-jabber.

EMAIL
No urgent action is required so an email will suffice.

1. SETTING UP THE MEETING

Send out a proper invite, ideally at least one day before the proposed time of the meeting. People need a chance to be prepared. However, in this case, as time is of the essence, schedule the meeting for later that afternoon. A proper meeting invite contains several key components:

→ **Title:** Pick a title that is descriptive—not something stupid like "Update." For example, "Discuss Brand XXX design client feedback."

→ **Purpose:** A brief description of the purpose of the meeting, for example, "Define the next steps for the Brand XXX logo design based on the recent client feedback."

→ **Time:** Keep it as short as possible. 30 minutes is usually all that's needed for most day-to-day project updates.

→ **Location:** This seems obvious, but is often forgotten.

→ **Invitees:** Keep the list of invitees as small as possible so as to not waste people's time. Don't invite people if they don't need to be there. If you're not sure, ask them or make their attendance optional.

→ **Set expectations:** Do people need to prepare anything for the meeting? Is there a feedback document they need to review? If so, this must be included in the invite.

THINGS <u>NOT</u> TO BRING TO A MEETING

EGOS

UNINFORMED OPINIONS

OFFICE DOGS

ITEMS NOT RELEVANT FOR THE MEETING TOPIC

UNNECESSARY PEOPLE

DISTRACTIONS

2. DURING THE MEETING

The organizer of the meeting is the de facto meeting owner. They are responsible for moderating the meeting (regardless of whether they are a senior project manager, a junior designer, or the Pope himself). A good meeting adheres to the following format:

→ **Outline the purpose of the meeting**

Begin every meeting with, "The purpose of this meeting is …" In our example, the purpose of the meeting is to "Define the next steps for the Brand XXX logo design based on the recent client feedback."

→ **Set expectations**

Communicate the desired outcome of this meeting. Is it to clarify the feedback from the client by gathering questions? Or is it simply to delegate the work packages to team members? Be clear and concrete.

→ **Be clear and concise**

Discuss the topic at hand in a clear and concise manner. No mindless jibber-jabber.

→ **Encourage questions**

Does anything need to be clarified? Creatives often don't ask questions in meetings, so the organizer should prompt individuals to ensure everything is crystal-clear.

→ **Define next steps and delegate tasks**

Define the concrete next steps and who is responsible for each of them. Everyone leaving the meeting should be clear as to exactly what is expected of them.

3. AFTER THE MEETING

The organizer sends out a short recap to the team that includes a summary of the meeting outcomes, the next steps, and the clearly defined roles and responsibilities so everyone knows what they are doing. This is often the most important part of the meeting, as your team will refer to this email for days to come as a point of reference.

Done all the above? Congratulations! You have mastered the art of efficient meeting running and would undoubtedly make even the most pedantic German proud.

MEETING ETIQUETTE

1. Clearly state the purpose of the meeting.
2. Keep the meeting as short as is humanly fucking possible.
3. Tell people in advance if they need to prepare or bring anything.
4. When explaining things, provide clear visual examples.
5. Do not act like a know-it-all and talk over people.
6. Avoid monologues, especially if you think you're clever (you're not).
7. Don't bring office dogs to meetings, they don't make you more creative.
8. Do not pick your nose.
9. Make sure everyone is clear on concrete next steps.
10. Send a follow-up recap after the meeting.

CUT OUT AND HANG IN MEETING ROOM

PITCHING

One of the most contentious practices when it comes to acquiring creative projects is the infamous free pitch, otherwise known as "spec work." If you've worked in an agency, or even as a freelancer, at some stage or another you'll probably have encountered this process of project acquisition wherein a prospective client sets a "test" brief to gauge the skills of their creative vendor. Of course, the controversial part of this practice is that these assignments are unpaid.

Free pitching has long been a part of the creative industries. In fact, research indicates that 70% of clients expect free "sample" work as part of the process of hiring an agency or a creative team[3]. For the larger agencies that can afford it, participating in free pitches is part and parcel of acquiring new clients. Larger agencies can afford to absorb these costs, so they do.

FREE PITCHING IN THE CREATIVE INDUSTRIES

When I worked in New York, every day one team or another at the agency would be neck deep in a pitch of some kind. Typically, the process for a pitch at a big agency starts with a "Request for Proposal (RFP)" arriving in the inbox of the agency's business development team. Once it has been decided that the agency will participate, a strategy and creative team are selected. They then hustle (usually in a short and intense period of time) to invent a creative solution to demonstrate the agency's skillset.

The timelines for pitches are usually insane. On some occasions you may have days, on others mere hours to create a fully formed creative approach (or multiple options, in some cases). Everyone hunkers down together in a war room and the creative team gets to dream up the next big idea without having to worry about production or budgetary realities. I remember one occasion when the creative team were briefed on the creative at 6pm on a Thursday evening with the client presentation scheduled for 1pm on the following day. Unbelievably, the work ended up being quite good and we won the pitch. It sounds crazy, and it usually is. But pitching can also be a lot of fun for a creative team.

IS PITCHING HELPFUL?

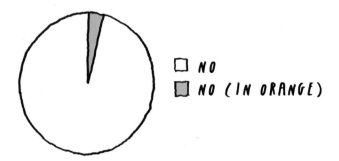

☐ NO
◼ NO (IN ORANGE)

---

[3] https://www.designweek.co.uk/issues/20-26-march-2017/research-reveals-70-clients-would-expect-designers-free-pitch/

RFP REQUIREMENTS

- ☐ We want.
- ☐ Free shit. Very cool shit.
- ☐ For free.
- ☐ Yep.
- ☐ Zero. Zilch. Null. Nada.
- ☐ ASAP.

THE CASE AGAINST FREE PITCHING

Despite its ubiquity in the creative industries, and fun as it is for a creative team who can afford it, many people regard free pitching as a questionable practice, and there has been significant movement against it in recent years. Many see it as an exploitative practice; in the design industry in particular, organizations including the AIGA[4] and NO!SPEC[5] have taken a public stand against it. Their argument is clear: There is no other industry on earth where you can expect a service provider to work for days or weeks for free just to aid a decision-making process. You would not expect a free "sample" meal from each of the five restaurants you're considering for dinner on Friday night. Why would you expect that when picking a designer or creative agency?

As a designer or agency, should one take the high road and say no to a free pitch? Or is this a utopian fantasy? Should you simply chalk up free pitching as "the cost of doing business," no different to taking a potential client to a fancy dinner?

WHY FREE PITCHING DOESN'T WORK

To be transparent with you, dear reader, it is the opinion of this author that free pitching is bad for the creative industries. It is a toxic practice that has simply become normalized over time. If you take a step back, the idea of giving a professional service away for free as a "trial run" is ridiculous. Not only that, but free pitching is not an effective evaluation process for the client. In short, free pitching works in nobody's favor. There are several reasons for this.

FREE PITCHING DEVALUES YOU AND YOUR WORK
By providing creative work in such a time crunch, with minimal briefing, and with little to no user research or client collaboration, you are creating a woefully skewed impression of what it takes to create great work. This grossly devalues you and your creative work.

[4] http://www.aiga.org/position-spec-work
[5] https://www.nospec.com

YOU RISK BEING RIPPED OFF

A client can simply appropriate any idea that is pitched and ask another agency or even their own in-house team to execute it more cheaply. I've seen this happen countless times.

FREE PITCHING COSTS MONEY AND RESOURCES

Although it is fine to pour money into business acquisition, the problem with free pitching is that you are investing money and resources into something that will likely be discarded. Pitch work takes time and energy away from real clients. It also sets bad habits for creative teams to just "make cool stuff" rather than think critically and solve problems.

Perhaps more important than this author's opinion or any creative industry view is the fact that creative pitching is also bad for the client. As fun as it is for creatives to create blue-sky solutions during the creative pitch, this method of evaluating an agency's skills is useless for the client. When a client asks you why pitching is bad for them, here are three reasons you can give them.

1: Pitch work does not demonstrate real problem-solving

Work produced in a pitch is usually impossible to execute and never considers production realities. Any design student can create "blue-sky" work; it is the execution of this work in the real world—with all the requirements and limitations—that requires true skill. If you, as a client, need a creative partner who can simply produce good pitch work, you would be better served getting a first-year design student who is good at making pretty Photoshop comps.

2: Pitch work is superficial

Pitch work almost never incorporates any real user research or discovery—key parts of creating meaningful work. To put it bluntly, it is superficial BS and, generally speaking, should be discarded after the pitch is over.

3: Pitch work won't tell you what it's like to work together

Most importantly, pitching does not involve collaboration with the client or their team—most of the time, the end result of the pitch is simply a presentation in front of the decision-making board. This gives no real indication of what it would be like to work together.

THE CHALLENGE WITH A "NO PITCH" POLICY

However, while protesting the free pitch may be good in theory, in practice, many clients will still want a free pitch. If you are an established creative or agency with a solid pipeline of inward new business leads it's easy to say

"Fuck you, we don't do pitches." When you are a smaller agency, a startup, a freelancer, or simply need the business, maintaining a hard line on this is not so easy. Creatives and agencies are faced with the dilemma: "Do we pitch and be part of the problem, or do we say no to free pitches and miss out on business?" It's a tricky question.

Let me give you an example. Edenspiekermann's Berlin office has a rigid "no pitch" policy. This is enshrined in a strongly worded manifesto[6] and, at least in theory, every word of it makes absolute sense. When I worked in the Berlin office, I dogmatically believed there was no situation where any sort of free pitch was a good situation. Of course, the Berlin office is a well-established agency in Europe. A few years later, when I returned to Edenspiekermann to run their new Los Angeles office, we had to approach things very differently. Unlike in Europe, the agency was virtually unknown in the US market, and getting new business was a challenge, especially at the start. My business partner and I had to seriously question whether we could make a utopian "no pitch" policy

> **"DO WE PITCH AND BE PART OF THE PROBLEM, OR DO WE SAY NO TO FREE PITCHES AND MISS OUT ON BUSINESS?"**

work in a new market where we were fighting for business tooth and nail. Throughout the first year of operating the business, we tried various ways to approach new business (including a couple of free pitches) and landed on an interesting alternative to the creative pitch: The creative debrief workshop.

THE CREATIVE DEBRIEF WORKSHOP

Whether you are a freelance designer or are running an agency, at some point you'll get an RFP project that you'd love to participate in, but requires the submission of free sample work to qualify. While you might have the most iron-clad no-pitch policy, the potential client will not budge on some sort of proof that you "get" their brand (despite your years of experience with similar projects), and you know that competing agencies will be submitting spec work. What do you do?

Enter the creative debrief workshop. Rather than following the lead of the competitors in the RFP, request a call with the decision-makers and explain to them how free pitching is not a good way to make an informed decision. Instead, you would like to offer them the chance to participate in

[6] www.edenspiekermann.com/manifesto

SHOULD I PITCH?

a creative debrief workshop on-site at their office. Rather than presenting a round of fake work over a 30-minute presentation, you'll use a full day of working together as a basis for them to evaluate what it is like to work with your team. Through a series of joint exercises in this workshop, you will explore the real business and user needs behind the creative assignment and produce something that is actually useful—even if they don't choose your agency ultimately.

In my first year at Edenspiekermann Los Angeles, we ran several of these workshops for proposals initially requesting pitch work, and we had a 100% success rate in closing the project after each of these working sessions. Clients got a real sense of what it was like to work with us, and also appreciated the fact that we were honest enough to tell them what they really needed.

HOW TO RUN A CREATIVE DEBRIEF WORKSHOP

Assuming you have convinced your prospective client that a creative debrief workshop is right for them, your team needs to prepare it. The overall theme of the creative debrief is "discovery and alignment." You want to find out as much as possible about the project and uncover user needs and insights that the client has not considered. By doing this process together over the course of a day, your chance of winning a pitch is far higher than if the agency simply submits spec work.

While the exact agenda of and exercises for each workshop will vary based on the respective project needs (a brand or campaign workshop would be quite different from a digital product workshop), here are some exercises to get you started.

During the workshop, it is important to start each exercise by explaining its purpose and outcomes. There are books filled with workshop methodologies and exercises (I highly recommend Jake Knapp's book *Sprint* by Google Ventures[7]), but regardless of the methods you use, each exercise in the creative debrief workshop needs to have a concrete outcome that is useful to the client (even if they don't choose your agency in the end).

---

[7] http://www.gv.com/sprint/

PERSONA DEFINITION EXERCISE

Time required: 120 minutes
Purpose: Define the target user groups for this project and understand what they actually need.

Preparation:
→ Blank persona cards printed on large sheets
→ One example of a fully completed persona card based on desk research
→ At least two persona archetypes to get things rolling if the group is stuck

Running the exercise:
→ The moderator starts the exercise by showing the example persona card to the group and then hangs it on the wall.
→ The moderator then asks the group what the next archetype should be. This first one will take the longest. The moderator provides prompts as needed to guide the exercises. Once each persona card is complete, the moderator hangs it on the wall.
→ After the first archetype is completed by the group, timebox each subsequent persona definition to 15 minutes.
→ Once the group feels that all main personas are covered, the group is invited to review the personas. No more than six personas should be produced. If more are created, then the group should critically examine these and consolidate them.

Outcome:
Completed persona cards for each main user group of the product/service.

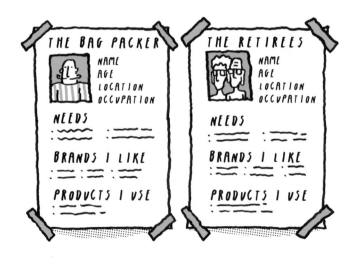

PRODUCT (OR BRAND) VISION BOARD EXERCISE

Time required: 120 minutes
Purpose: Identify opportunities for the product or brand for each user group.

Preparation:
→ Divide a large wall space into a matrix of six columns and three rows.
→ Hang persona cards from the previous exercise at the top of each column.
→ To the left of each row is a label. From top to bottom, the labels read: "Needs," "Solutions," and "Values."

Running the exercise:
→ Persona by persona, the moderator asks the group what each user needs based on the context of the product or brand. For example, if this was a food-finding app, it could be "I need a way to see if the food I'm eating is suitable for diabetics."
→ Once the "Needs" box for that persona is complete, the moderator moves on to "Solutions." For each "Need" there should be a corresponding solution. For the previous food app example, a solution for the need would be: "A filter that allows me to only show food suitable for diabetics."
→ The final step is "Values," where, based on the solutions, you write what value the solution adds to people's lives. Using the same example again, a value could be "this food-finding app is my way to find great food regardless of my dietary needs."

Outcome:
Product/brand vision board showing needs and corresponding opportunities.

PAGE TYPES EXERCISE

Time required: 90+ minutes (depending on the scale of the digital product)
Purpose: Define the pages (or screens) in a website or app project, what their purpose is, and what elements they contain.

Preparation:
→ Enough printouts of the blank page type template so that each participant in the workshop can map out all the primary pages.

Running the exercise:
→ The moderator explains the exercise and gathers a list of all pages that will be brainstormed in this session. There should be no more than 15 in a work session. Only the main pages of the site are included; tertiary pages such as legal disclosures, or "standard" pages that will not require an extensive thinking exercise (e.g., an off-the-shelf contact page or a standard FAQ page) are not included.
→ The group is divided into teams of two and the pages are divided between the teams.
→ In a timebox of 30 minutes, the group completes the page type templates for their assigned pages.
→ Each team presents their completed page templates for discussion.
→ The results and the discussion are documented by the moderator on the templates.

Outcome:
A consolidated map of the pages on the website.

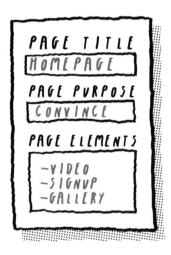
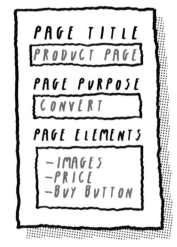

VISUAL VOCABULARY EXERCISE

Time required: 120 minutes
Purpose: Create alignment on the visual language.

Outcome:
A concrete alignment on the visual direction of the brand, campaign, or product.

(See page 71 for a full breakdown on running this exercise.)

FREE PITCHING: A SLOW CHANGE

As long as there are agencies and clients, free pitching will probably always be part of the creative industries to some extent. If we want to change this, we as an industry have a responsibility to educate our clients about why unpaid creative work isn't good for the work or their business. Regardless of whether you convince them otherwise, there is an opportunity to educate a client every time a request for unpaid work comes in. Free pitching has been part and parcel of the client–agency culture for decades, so if we want to change how things are done, this responsibility falls to us.

SCOPING

Some of the worst practices of the creative industries—long hours, rushed work, frayed nerves, and general chaos—often have one root cause: a badly scoped project. It might be too little budget, too short a timeline, or a list of unachievable deliverables.

When it comes to scoping projects, we creatives are often our own worst enemy. For us, when a project seems creatively exciting, all measurement of reality can go out the window. We rush the preparation of the scope, saying yes to pretty much anything the client asks for just to win the project. Many times in my early career I said to a potential client, "Let's just do it and we'll figure out the details later!" Of course, two months down the road, this bit us on the ass every time.

Accounts people and those in business development, whose salaries depend (at least partially) on selling projects, are also frequently responsible for poor project scopes, underestimating how much effort it will take to get a project done due to lack of knowledge, or simply not giving a shit once the money is in the door.

Regardless of who is to blame for a bad scope, everybody suffers. Overpromising may win the project, but it almost always ends with stress, underdelivering, and long hours—in short, a disappointed client and a pissed-off team.

THE PROBLEMS WITH BAD SCOPING

At some stage or another in our careers, most of us will learn the lesson of a badly scoped project. Usually it only takes one incident to make us think carefully before saying yes to every whim of the client the next time. A couple of years ago, I made the mistake on a very big project for a Fortune 500 company. The project was a large corporate website redesign and build, and would run for several months. There was a huge budget involved. In the rush to close the deal, we hurriedly gathered our team and wrote a project scope and proposal under the assumption that "It's a big budget, it will be fine!" In hindsight, it was anything but—and it wouldn't take long before this scope would come back to screw us.

REGARDLESS OF WHO IS TO BLAME FOR A BAD SCOPE, EVERYBODY SUFFERS.

The document was vague and best described as a blank check that promised to deliver any random idea that popped into our client's head. Unsurprisingly, the client was delighted with the proposal, and the project was signed off. Our happiness was short-lived. Within mere weeks of the project starting, we realized there was a mountain of legacy system architecture that we would have to decipher for weeks or even months before we wrote one line of code.

The last weeks of the project were truly a living hell. Trying to cram a mountain of features into a legacy system, combined with unrelenting client feedback, was like being forced to drink from a firehose while riding a unicycle. The last month featured 60-hour weeks and a very unhappy team on the verge of quitting.

In a group retrospective after the conclusion of the project, our team identified that all of this could have been avoided had the project been scoped correctly from the start. The lesson: Taking the time to scope a

HOW SHOULD I PRICE A PROJECT?

Start here → **TYPE OF PROJECT**

FIXED DEADLINE | **SMALL DIGITAL PROJECT** | **ONGOING PROJECT** | **LARGE DIGITAL PROJECT**

HAVE YOU INVOLVED ALL COMPETENCES IN PLANNING?

YES **NO**

HAVE YOU DEFINED EXACT, QUANTIFIABLE DELIVERABLES?

YES **NO**

DON'T SKIP THIS STEP

FIXED-PRICE SCOPE

Projects of a known quantity are suitable for fixed-price scoping because of their predictability.

RETAINER

For ongoing work, a retainer can be a good choice as the client can adjust their deliverables in a set budget.

AGILE PROJECT

Due to unknowns and sheer complexity, large digital projects are extremely difficult to scope in a fixed price.

creative project properly is crucial. Once signed, a bad scope cannot be easily fixed and the creative team working on it are pretty much stuck with whatever ridiculous timeline was predefined (often without their input). Not only that, but a poorly defined scope locks you into a slew of problems.

IT CAUSES LONG HOURS

Badly scoped projects are one of the main reasons for long hours in the creative industries. Almost without exception, when a project is badly scoped it means a hustle at the end to meet the deadline.

A POORLY DEFINED SCOPE ALWAYS RESULTS IN MORE WORK THAN ORIGINALLY BUDGETED

IT DEVALUES THE WORK

A poorly defined scope always results in more, never less, work than originally budgeted for. This in turn devalues the work by literally pushing down the price-per-line item over the course of the project. The worst part is, once a client has successfully squeezed more from a scope once, rest assured they will do it again. In some extreme cases, this means ending a relationship with a client because you have given them such a skewed understanding of how much creative work should cost.

THE QUALITY SUFFERS

When you're in a rush simply to get the work done, it doesn't take a genius to realize that the quality suffers. While the occasional rushed project is fine, making a habit of this means you become the creative or agency doing mediocre work. When someone deciding whether to hire you looks at your portfolio, they don't give a shit if it took you two hours or two months to make that piece of work—they just care how good it is.

IT COSTS MONEY

Even if you don't care about your team or the quality of the work, bad scoping costs money. When you are locked into a poorly scoped project and scrambling to complete everything on time, you will inevitably throw more people at the task or bring in freelancers just to get it done. Unsurprisingly, more people equals more costs.

FIXED-PRICE
VS. AGILE SCOPING

There are two main ways to price a creative project: Either the client buys deliverables, or they buy time. Each method has clear pros and cons.

Deliverable-based fixed-price scoping is probably still the most common way to price a creative project. The fixed-price scope is simple: "You pay me X and you get Y." On the surface, there are clear benefits to a fixed price. The client knows exactly what they are getting, and the creative or agency has a fixed amount of guaranteed income for a body of work. However, below the surface, the fixed-price model has a big issue: inflexibility. A fixed price is a fixed price. That makes any scope change that may occur spontaneously during the course of a project very difficult. It requires going back to the scope, adjusting, and going through the whole approval process again.

A fixed price and the according deliverables is decided when there is the least amount of information available—i.e., before a project even starts. This is not usually an issue for a project like a brand design or a campaign with a fixed number of deliverables. However, when it comes to a digital product or anything with technology—something that is prone to constant change—a fixed scope can become a major problem. How can anyone make a realistic estimate about how long a specific feature will take to implement before the technology stack is agreed on? Fixed prices for complex digital products are in trouble from the start and should be avoided at all costs.

The second way of scoping a creative project is where the client buys time. There are different ways of formulating this, from simply billing by the hour to fixed retainers where the client buys X number of hours per month. The issue with time-based billing is the lack of clarity—the client doesn't quite know what they're getting, and the creative or agency doesn't know exactly how much work is expected or guaranteed so it is harder to plan. However, the advantage is clear for both sides—buying time means that changes can be easily incorporated without adjusting lengthy and often complex scope documents.

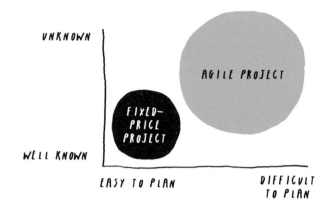

THE AGILE APPROACH TO SCOPING

A hybrid model between the fixed-price and time-based approaches is agile scoping. The client still has the security of working within a fixed price, but instead of buying a fixed set of deliverables, the client works together with the creatives to define a general outline of what the project should achieve within the "bought time." This is especially suitable for digital products, where assigning an exacting list of deliverables can be hazardous.

An agile pricing model gives the client the flexibility of swapping items at any stage in the project without additional cost (providing that it still falls within the time budgeted). In addition, this approach embraces change by incorporating learning throughout the project and allowing the team to adjust course accordingly.

Let's say, for example, that you're working on a booking app for a travel company. Halfway through the project, after the first beta release, a round of user feedback comes in. These insights indicate that users want to see more real images of hotels, perhaps even integrating Instagram content into the app. On the other hand, it seems virtually nobody has engaged with the messaging functionality. In an agile project, you can easily embrace these findings and reprioritize work accordingly, focusing on the Instagram integration and pushing back any further development on the messaging system without having to write a new proposal.

This approach requires a significant amount of trust, so it works best with a client with whom you have a good relationship. If you can get your client to buy into the idea of an agile scope, this is by far the best approach to pricing, and producing, a successful long-term digital project.

HOW TO SCOPE A
FIXED-PRICE PROJECT

Although an agile approach to scoping a project may be your preferred method, the vast majority of proposals in the creative industries are still fixed-price; in many cases, the client will insist on it. If you must use the fixed-price approach, taking the time to prepare a well-considered scope will save time, money, and bucketloads of stress in the long run.

INVOLVE ALL REPRESENTATIVES
It may seem like a no-brainer, but be sure to involve representatives of all the disciplines that will work on the project. In my experience, the most glaring—and mind-boggling—omissions from scoping processes is the technology team; often the most significant part of a project. Take the time and involve all parties, from copywriters to developers, to get input on the project scope.

GET INPUT FROM THE PEOPLE ACTUALLY DOING THE WORK
Just as important as having all the various disciplines weigh in, ask the actual team that will be working on the project to weigh in, not the senior representatives of each department. A caveat here is that the more junior the individuals, the more time they think they need, so their input should be weighed accordingly.

PLAN FOR THE WORST CASE
Murphy's Law says that "whatever can go wrong, will go wrong." In a creative project, this reads as "whatever can go wrong, will go wrong, and then the client will change it all anyway." Include a minimum 10% buffer time in all projects to allow for unexpected developments.

BE PAINFULLY SPECIFIC
If you are working with a fixed-price scope with fixed deliverables, there is no such thing as being too granular when scoping a project. The document should state exactly what is and is not included, how many rounds of feedback, when, and in what format.

BE SURE TO SPECIFY WHAT'S NOT INCLUDED
Typically, items such as stock images, font licenses, commissioning photographers or illustrations, and travel costs are not included in your price. When writing your scope, be sure to specify any third-party or additional costs that are not included in the price.

WRITING A FIXED-PRICE SCOPE

A well-written fixed-price scope is usually a lengthy document, and for good reason. A fixed-price scope should contain the following elements.

1: DESCRIPTION OF EACH PHASE OF WORK
As well as listing each phase, be sure to outline what the purpose is. For example, for a "Logo concept phase," the description would be "Define a range of concepts from which the client will select one."

2: DELIVERABLES
When providing deliverables, be specific to a fault. For example:

→ We will create three logo directions that will be presented to the client in person at their office.
→ For the concept presentation, each direction will be mocked up in three sample applications: app loading screen, business card, and letterhead.
→ Following the presentation, the client will choose one direction. If one of these logos is not deemed suitable, the agency can provide additional directions on a time and materials basis.
→ The client will provide one round of feedback on the chosen logo concept. Any additional feedback rounds can be provided on a time and materials basis.
→ All feedback will be delivered in writing. In addition, a representative from the client should be available for a phone call to clarify any feedback questions that might arise.
→ Approval on final concept will be provided in writing.

3: COSTS
For full transparency, break these down by hours (or days, depending on what the client prefers) and include a breakdown of the different roles working on each phase.

4: TIMELINE
Every scope proposal needs to include a timeline of deliverables and, most importantly, when feedback is due. In addition, be sure to include a sentence that states that late feedback will have a knock-on effect on later deadlines.

FIXED-SCOPE CALCULATOR

DAY RATE
The baseline factor.

DAYS SOLD
A fair estimation based on a discussion with all of the different competences that will be involved in the project.

DIFFICULT CLIENT (+5%)
Expect endless feedback rounds? Factor it in.

RUSHED WORK (+5%)
No one should have to work weekends. Charge for that shit.

UNCLEAR DELIVERABLES (+10%)
Better still, clarify the details and save time and money.

TECH UNCERTAINTIES (+10%)
Unknown tech is a black hole, and needs to be factored in. Ideally it is better to use a time-based calculation.

TOTAL:

BRIEFINGS

I used to work with a creative director—let's call him Andrew Arugulaoff—who lived his life by the mantra "No brief? No work." He was dogmatic about this to a fault. Want to design a new loading screen for an app? Write a brief. Want to change the typeface on a poster? Write a brief. Want to lighten the color of a button? Write a fucking brief. Such was his belief in this mantra that I wouldn't have been surprised if this slogan were tattooed on his buttocks. Andrew's slogan was legendary in the agency and, much to the delight of the entire creative department, it used to drive the accounts people crazy.

While this dogmatic approach may seem a little extreme, I cannot overstate the importance of proper briefings in any project. All too often, creatives are rushed into producing work without a proper briefing. Working without a briefing, or with a bad one, is inefficient and costs time. It sets work on the wrong path from the start.

Whether you are a freelancer working on your own, a junior designer at an agency, an in-house product designer, or even a creative overlord, there is no assignment that will not benefit from taking 30 minutes to write a proper briefing. Regardless of how small it may be, or even if it is just for yourself, every creative task needs a clear objective and list of deliverables defined before work begins. No brief? No work.

BAD BRIEFINGS ARE FOR ASSHOLES

A briefing can literally make or break a creative project. Do it well, and you can work efficiently, produce work that is on-strategy, meets the client's expectations, and, most importantly, everyone can go home on time. Fail to brief correctly and a shitshow of off-strategy creative work, late hours, and a disappointed client are sure to follow. Despite all of this, bad briefings are still surprisingly common in the creative industries. Given the fast pace and tight deadlines we often operate with, sometimes an assignment seems too small and the timeline too short to "waste time" on a creative brief. This will bite you on the ass every time.

Let me give you an example. A few years ago, I worked on a content retainer for a large corporate client. "Content retainer" is a fancy way of saying that once a week we would source a featured image for the new article on their blog. Given the seemingly "simple" nature of this task, there was no senior leadership on the project and no real briefing given. Instead, one lucky designer would be assigned to create the image of the week, and would usually spend days scouring Getty Images looking for something that would convey an abstract topic such as "MOB spread" (yes, that is a real thing). It was a mess. Because the tasks were never briefed, the designer spent half the time figuring out what the hell "MOB spread" meant and then the rest of the time desperately trying to find a way to convey it by going into a Getty Images clickhole until midnight every day. Week in, week out, the retainer burned through so much budget that it was actually costing us money to work on the project.

A BRIEFING CAN LITERALLY MAKE OR BREAK A CREATIVE PROJECT.

Eventually, the whole thing came to a head and it was clear the process needed to change or we needed to stop the project. The aforementioned creative director on the account—a very experienced individual—saw the ensuing chaos and, after sternly reprimanding the account team,

TO BRIEF OR NOT TO BRIEF...

PROPER BRIEFING

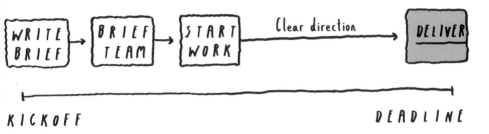

WRITE BRIEF → BRIEF TEAM → START WORK —— Clear direction ——→ DELIVER

KICKOFF   DEADLINE

NO BRIEFING

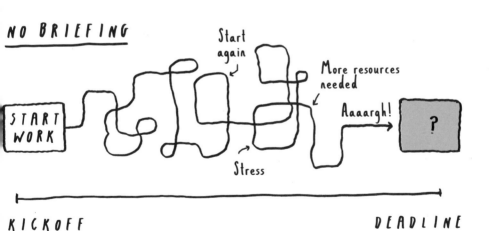

Start again

More resources needed

START WORK

Aaaargh!

?

Stress

KICKOFF   DEADLINE

stepped into the project. There would be no more aimless days going down the Getty Images clickhole. Instead, each image selection assignment would start with a proper brief to fully understand and identify the themes of the respective topic, followed by a short brainstorming session to define the three concepts the designer would pursue. Doing the briefing meeting added just one hour at the start of the week while saving days in image searching. Not only that, but the difference in the quality of the output was like night and day. I worked on a few of these images myself, and I am still proud of the results—due in no small part to the good briefings.

BAD BRIEFINGS

All too often, creative briefs are given verbally or are simply not specific enough. A bad briefing usually suffers from one of the following common problems:

→ The briefing is not written down or is nonexistent.
→ There is no in-person briefing meeting where creatives can ask questions.
→ The briefing document is too long.
→ Concrete expectations and deliverables—and who is responsible for them—are not clear.
→ Deadlines are not clear.

HOW TO BRIEF A PROJECT CORRECTLY

There are two key components to a good project briefing: An in-person kickoff where questions can be addressed, and a follow-up written brief that can be used as a constant reference for the creative team as they work through the project.

TAKE A STEP BACK AND WRITE A BRIEF
No matter how small the project, how much of a rush you're in, or how tight your deadline, you will always save time by being prepared. A briefing might take a couple of hours to prepare and execute, but a lack of one can cost you days or even weeks.

GOOD BRIEF	BAD BRIEF

WRITTEN	VERBAL ONLY

CLEAR BULLET POINTS	RAMBLING PROSE

CLEAR DEADLINES	NO DEADLINE

EVEN IF YOU HAVE A BRIEF FROM THE CLIENT, DO A REBRIEFING

Even if you have a briefing from the client, in most cases it makes sense to rewrite it. This is called a rebriefing and is more than a formatting exercise; it's about structuring and prioritizing their needs in a way that gets the best from your creative team.

DO AN IN-PERSON BRIEFING TOO

In addition to the written briefing, it is always important to do an in-person (or via phone) briefing. There is no substitute for a session where the client or account team can directly convey what goals the creative work needs to achieve, as well as clarifying any questions from the creatives working on the project.

ENCOURAGE QUESTIONS

Creative people are notoriously quiet when it comes to questions. Prod and poke them until they ask what is actually on their mind.

HOW TO WRITE A GREAT BRIEFING DOCUMENT

Writing a great briefing document is far from rocket science. In fact, it follows an idiot-proof formula that can be reused for virtually any project. The document is short and clear, uses bullet points instead of paragraphs, and is not more than two pages long—creatives will glaze over if it is any longer. There are different ways to formulate a brief, but in general they follow this overall structure.

BACKGROUND

The background to this assignment helps us to understand why the client is doing this project. Maybe there is a new competitor on the market which means they need to run a new campaign. Or perhaps a recent round of user feedback has indicated that the homescreen of their app needs to be rethought. This is usually a paragraph or two and is generally the most verbose part of the briefing (and, therefore, most likely to be ignored by the designers).

ASSIGNMENT

What exactly is it that we need to do? This should be no more than one line; the detailed deliverables will be listed later.

ANATOMY OF A GOOD BRIEF

BRIEFING

BACKGROUND — Context of the assignment

ASSIGNMENT — One-line description of the project

OBJECTIVES — What business goals does it need to fulfill?

DELIVERABLES — A list of concrete deliverables

DEADLINES — Both internal and external deadlines

RESOURCES — Links to files, documents, etc.

OBJECTIVES

If there are concrete business goals or user goals that this assignment needs to solve, they should be listed here. Do we want to increase sales? Or make it easier for users to access their accounts? These points should be specific and quantifiable.

THE STRATEGY

This one is a must-have for ad campaigns or brand projects. It outlines the central communication or brand message we need to convey, otherwise known as "The Big Idea." For example, it could be: "Fluffy is the softest on the market" for a campaign for a new toilet paper brand that is extra-gentle on the bottom.

DELIVERABLES

These should be outlined with concise bullet points definitively listing exactly what needs to be produced. No fluff here; this needs to be the sharpest part of the brief. For example, exactly how many versions of the concept need to be presented? What ad sizes are required?

DEADLINES

The briefing should detail not only the final deadline, but all the various milestones along the way—internal reviews, first client presentation, final presentation of revised designs, and final production deadline.

RESOURCES

List any additional resources. Be specific as to the purpose of including each of these resources in the briefing and make it crystal clear what is required reading and what is optional reading. There is nothing worse than getting a list of five encyclopedia-length books in a briefing document and wondering what the hell you need to do with them. In addition, if there are any examples that help illustrate your point, be sure to include them here. Again, be clear as to why these examples are included. If you include an app design that has solved a similar challenge in a novel way, be sure to highlight what that feature is. For example: "Check out the Instagram app for how you can switch to different profiles within the same app."

VISUAL BRIEFINGS

Given the visual nature of creative work, sometimes a written briefing isn't enough. A non-visual client will rarely be able to articulate how their project should look and feel. This usually means producing many concept directions in the hope that one of them will hit the mark with the client. However, there is another way to get even the most non-visual client to give a briefing that vastly reduces the amount of guesswork, therefore producing work that is more likely to hit the mark from the start. This technique is the "visual vocabulary exercise."

The visual vocabulary exercise is a hands-on session that helps determine the direction for the visual language. It centers around a large-scale "visual wall" of curated reference material that has been prepared in advance. The client (or group of clients) removes, exchanges, and annotates items on the wall and then explains why they left certain items on the wall (e.g. "This font feels like us because it is modern"). The purpose of the exercise is to give the client a way to share their gut feeling on how their brand or product should look and feel, even if they do not have the verbal vocabulary to express it. For example, not all clients have the design knowledge to say "our brand should use a serif font so that we feel more institutional."

GIVEN THE VISUAL NATURE OF CREATIVE WORK, SOMETIMES A WRITTEN BRIEFING ISN'T ENOUGH.

The exercise requires quite a bit of preparation in advance, but is a lot less effort than spinning your wheels for weeks on dozens of creative directions that the client may or may not like. What is important to stress is that the visual vocabulary is not a moodboard. It is a highly focused matrix to get a sense of where the client sees their brand or product positioned in a visual landscape of infinite possibilities. Combined with an in-person kickoff and a great written document, it is the most direct and useful briefing you can ever give a creative.

THE VISUAL VOCABULARY EXERCISE

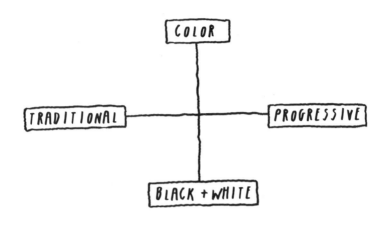

1. DEFINE THE AXIS

3. CLIENTS REMOVE ITEMS THAT DON'T FIT THEIR BRAND

2. BUILD A VISUAL WALL OF REFERENCE MATERIAL

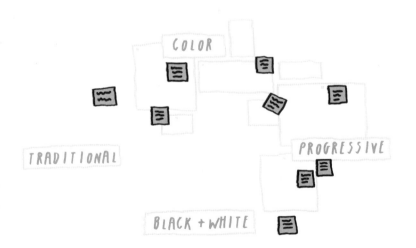

4. DISCUSSION NOTES ARE THE BASIS OF CREATIVE BRIEFS

FEEDBACK

The creative industries are rife with colorful stories of famous individuals who, during the course of a project, come in and decide to tear down weeks of work and start again in the quest for "greatness." This is, of course, part of any good process that wishes to produce quality work. However, in my experience, creative leadership often has difficulty with giving useful feedback to their teams.

Clear, unambiguous feedback is critical to producing great work. This doesn't mean being a dick, but it does mean being honest, clear, and direct. Creative directors often forget that what is crystal clear to them may not be for the junior designer with vastly less experience. This results in both a frustrated designer and a creative director who simply cannot understand why the other one doesn't "get it."

In my first years as a design director, I would meet the design team to give my two cents on their design solutions. I would give feedback like, "Needs to be bolder!" or "Let's make it more epic," which, in hindsight, is baffling: It was unclear, unspecific, and completely useless. A good leader caters to the lowest common denominator—the least knowledgeable junior—when it comes to giving a briefing or feedback. If that person doesn't understand, your feedback is useless. When the next round of work comes back looking like shit, it is your fault, not theirs.

HOW NOT TO GIVE FEEDBACK

There is a second, less likable, group of creative leaders who are also notoriously bad when it comes to giving feedback. They are none other than our lovable old friend, the egomaniac. The egomaniac likes to use the opportunity of giving feedback as an ego-building exercise. They get to stand up in front of shy juniors and sound "clever." They get to regale the ready-made audience with their tales of wisdom from the "good old days." Above all, they feel like they have cemented their relevance in a world where their skills are rapidly going the way of the dinosaurs. There is nothing more ridiculous (and, quite frankly, embarrassing) than a fifty-five-year-old man who has never owned a smartphone standing at the top of a room preaching to a highly skilled twenty-six-year-old digital designer about what makes a good mobile-user experience. Yet it happens every day. In fact, if you work at a big agency, it's probably happening in your building this very second.

Most agencies have at least one egomaniac creative director who loves nothing more than the sound of their own voice. The most memorable that I've ever met was an executive creative director—let's call her Gertrude Gringlegoggles—at a big agency. Gertrude was a very nasty piece of work.

CLEAR UNAMBIGUOUS FEEDBACK IS CRITICAL TO PRODUCING GREAT WORK. THIS DOESN'T MEAN BEING A DICK

I encountered Gertrude on a large project that both of our teams were working on together. Gertrude was an unsmiling woman with a background in advertising, and was some 30-odd years into her career. She led a large team of talented creatives but, given the way she treated them, I was surprised she had a single employee. She was a tyrant to everyone, and this behavior was most apparent when it came to giving feedback.

Gertrude liked to have an audience when delivering feedback. She would invite all team members to a meeting in the largest conference room available. The work was projected onto the screen and everyone would take their seats. The team would sit around tensely as she would glare at the work on screen, the only audible sounds in the room being the hum of the projector and the heavy breathing of Gertrude. After what felt like an eternity, Gertrude would clear her throat, and in a cracked voice not dissimilar to that of Sauron, say, "Who made the buttons green?" The room would freeze in a terrified silence. I didn't even work for this woman and I nearly shat myself. From the corner of the room, one of her team slowly raised his hand,

THE DREADED FEEDBACK LOOP

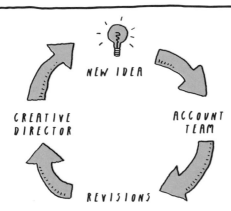

NEW IDEA

CREATIVE
DIRECTOR

ACCOUNT
TEAM

REVISIONS

(Repeat this process until one minute before deadline. Fun!)

knowing full well what was in store. "Green is the client's brand color and they insist …," he would begin to stutter before being cut down by Gertrude. "Are you stupid? Green is a hateful color. It is the color of vomit. Do you want the user to vomit? This page looks like you vomited it out of your mouth, you fucking idiot!"

Gertrude would rise unsteadily to her feet, turn to face the design team, and begin one of her famous rants. "Do you know nothing about creative? All you care about is making things that work! You don't care about the idea. When I created the most successful ad campaign of all time in 1986, we made things that were unforgettable! UNFORGETTABLE. Does this crap look unforgettable to you?!" She would point at the screen. I didn't like to say it at the time, but it was not the team's goal to make the "report error" form on the screen unforgettable.

By and large, our team was shielded from Gertrude's wrath. However, on one occasion, close to the launch of the project, I received an email from her with feedback for our team. The email was in barely coherent English. It read like an angry note from a six-year-old. Certain phrases that Gertrude obviously felt were of particular importance were highlighted for extra impact. "Are you stupid?" and "This is embarrassing!" were two of my favorites. Of course, the feedback contained no actionable items and was useless other than as a rant. Our team would sit together after these sessions and attempt to interpret the intent behind the tirade. After all, how does one make the UI design of a contact form less embarrassing? If the project was not already in its final week before launch, I would have told Gertrude exactly where she could shove it.

What people like Gertrude tend to forget is that the real purpose of giving feedback is twofold. Firstly, and most obviously, it is to drive innovation and get the best possible result from a team. However, there is a second success factor when it comes to feedback: Team growth. Good feedback is a learning opportunity so that a team learns how to do it themselves the next time. The egomaniac usually doesn't give a shit about the second part.

Now, let's be clear: I am certainly not suggesting that giving feedback is supposed to be a feelgood exercise. Quite the contrary. Without direct and honest feedback, we would live in a world filled with mediocrity, boring work, and zero innovation. Direct and honest feedback is critical to having a team that produces great work. However, regardless of whether feedback is good or bad, the most important aspect is to explain why this respective feedback was given. Otherwise, how can you expect a team to grow? Negative feedback is a great learning opportunity, provided it is delivered in a constructive manner. When an egomaniac comes in and yells "Start again!" without any sort of rationale other than "it's not good enough," what sort of learning experience is that for a team?

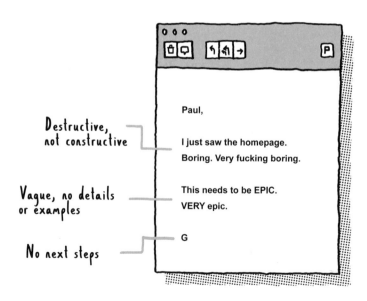

Destructive,
not constructive

Vague, no details
or examples

No next steps

Paul,

I just saw the homepage.
Boring. Very fucking boring.

This needs to be EPIC.
VERY epic.

G

THE DOS AND DON'TS OF GIVING FEEDBACK

Here's how you can deliver even the most scathing feedback without being an asshole (and have your team learn something along the way).

BE DIRECT AND HONEST

Don't sugarcoat feedback. Be direct and honest at all times. A creative director who sugarcoats feedback will almost certainly produce mediocre work. Be polite and respectful, but straight to the point and uncompromising. Never feel guilty or afraid to make people start again.

BE POSITIVE AND CONSTRUCTIVE

The egomaniac never wants to cede their power or control to others, which is why they make such bad leaders. A good creative leader's job is not only to produce great work, but to build teams that can produce great work by themselves. When you give feedback, ask yourself whether your team will learn from this experience. Building a great team means building the skills and confidence of individuals with constructive feedback. Creatives work best when they feel safe to make mistakes and experiment without fearing the wrath of an overpowering leader.

BE CLEAR AND UNAMBIGUOUS

This is where creative leaders, even those with the very best of intentions, often fall short. Your feedback should be clear and, above all, actionable. Good feedback is concrete and leaves no room for ambiguity. Instead of a vague statement like "The homepage needs to be more epic," be clear: "The lack of images and white background on the homepage makes the design too boring and plain. Let's try a looping background video in the top hero area. Also, let's try a version where you invert the background colors on the page so it has more impact."

PROVIDE EXAMPLES

Verbal or written feedback, no matter how explicit, is not always enough. Always provide an example of the point you wish to make. In our previous "boring homepage" example, here you could show a great example of a background video to illustrate the exact look you desire.

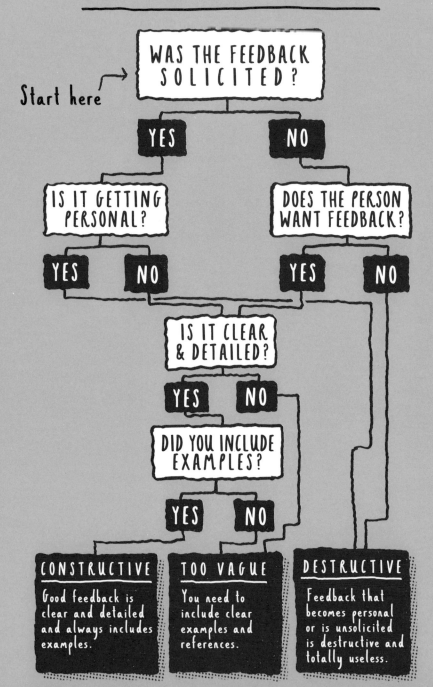

ENCOURAGE QUESTIONS

It's all too common that creatives—especially juniors—are afraid to ask questions in case they sound stupid. The creative leader who makes their team feel stupid about asking questions is the real idiot in the room. Ensure your team feels secure by including a dedicated segment for questions in every feedback session and not closing it until every creative in the room has asked at least one question.

THE DOS AND DON'TS OF TAKING FEEDBACK

Just as a creative or design director has a responsibility to deliver clear and constructive feedback, creatives also need to interpret it correctly in order to produce great work. For the creatives reading this, here's how to keep your side of the bargain.

READ THE BRIEF

This may seem like the most obvious thing in the world, but it never fails to surprise me. You're not in university anymore—thoroughly understanding the assignment is not an optional activity. Read the fucking brief, please.

NOW READ THE BRIEF AGAIN

Yes, you heard me right. You probably missed something, most likely in the Deliverables section. Please read it again.

ASK QUESTIONS

For some reason, many creatives seem to think that asking questions makes them look stupid. They keep silent in briefing sessions and only ask their peers what something meant much later on. Remember this: There are no stupid questions, only stupid people who don't ask any questions. If you don't know something, then ask.

TAKE NOTES

This is my pet hate, and is extremely common among junior creatives and interns. You are not a superhero with a photographic memory: Take fucking notes. On paper, with a pen.

SECRET TOOLS FOR TAKING FEEDBACK

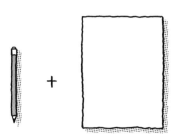

PRESENTATIONS

There comes a time in the life of every creative project where the work leaves the safety of the creator's MacBook and is put in front of a client ("client" also refers to internal stakeholders if you are working at an in-house company) for judgment. While presenting work is easy for the lucky few, for most creatives—especially junior ones—the idea of standing in front of a room of people and talking for 30 minutes straight fills us with dread. Palms get sweaty and throats suddenly become dry. We long for the floor to open up and swallow us into an abyss.

Allow me to let you in on a little-known fact about creative presentations: No matter how much of a smooth talker the account person or the creative director is, they can never present as well as the person who actually made the work. A great presentation is not a sales job; it's about guiding a client through the thought process and rationale behind a creative solution. It doesn't matter if you lack a Steve Jobs-style on-stage persona and fumble your words. The fact is, the person who actually knows what they're talking about will always come across as if they know what they're talking about, regardless of delivery. No amount of sales BS can compensate for actual knowledge. However, as with everything, there is a right way and a wrong way to present creative work.

THE "BIG REVEAL"
APPROACH TO PRESENTATIONS

Traditionally, creative presentations were set up like a Vegas-style magic show. The puppet master—usually the creative director—would lead a group of wide-eyed clients through a dramatic "big reveal" of the creative work. After dozens of "inspiring" presentation slides and an inevitable monologue from the creative director, the great moment would arrive when the work was unveiled. No expense would be spared in these presentations. Every trick in the book—flashy motion graphics, emotional mood videos, epic background music, dancing kittens in leotards—would be employed to sell the piece of creative work. These occasions were quite a show and probably the highlight of the egomaniac's year.

One of the most famous showmen I have heard of was an infamous creative director, now retired; let's call him Arthur Albatross. A true 1950s ad man, Arthur took the "big reveal" ritual very seriously, employing maximum showmanship to wow the client. His party trick was to use a giant antique steel case, not unlike something a magician would own. The case was so large that he could have stowed at least two bodies inside it. For every presentation, large or small, Arthur would wheel this monstrosity into the client's office. You could hear it rattling down the hallway from the other side of the building. When the moment came, Arthur would wheel the case to the front of the presentation room. A pause for dramatic effect would follow. Arthur would then take a deep breath and, in one swift movement, and with surprising strength, hoist the case onto the conference table with a thunderous impact. The violent motion would cause glassware to rattle and pens to roll off, to the sound of gasps from any clients who were new to the show. Dead silence followed for at least five seconds. Then, in a deep, dramatic voice (not dissimilar to Morgan Freeman), Arthur would begin his monologue. With the audience's eyes firmly glued to the closed steel case, he would slowly explain the Big Idea, lingering on every detail. After one last dramatic pause, he would unlock the case with a low creaking sound. Between two sheets of glass, like an ancient Egyptian artifact, would be a pristine print of the ad concept he was selling that day. The clients would go nuts for it. In truth, you could have put a dog turd behind those sheets of glass and they still would have applauded.

Of course, in order to get to this dramatic moment, there was the small

TRADITIONALLY, CREATIVE PRESENTATIONS WERE SET UP LIKE A VEGAS-STYLE MAGIC SHOW.

task of producing the work itself. In traditional agencies, this is usually done by a group of much more junior creatives who remained hidden behind the curtain, never to interact with the client. In fact, it is common that the creative director is not involved at all, except for the final presentation. Weeks or months before the Big Reveal, the client would commission the assignment and a brief would be written. Much like reclusive medieval monks, the creative team would then lock themselves in a dark cave to begin on this wondrous conceptual work of art. After weeks, or even months, they would emerge from the tomb like a modern-day Jesus, carrying aloft the next Big Idea that would transform their client's business.

Now, while there is no disputing that the "big reveal" approach is certainly entertaining and would brighten up the afternoon of any client, it was hit or miss in terms of delivering great work. Given that creatives are not modern-day Messiahs and lack mind-reading powers, the "big reveal" approach has about a 50/50 chance of producing a creative solution that the client doesn't like or even need. As fun as it is to work in a black box for weeks on end, the exclusion of the client—the person who knows their business best—is not the smartest way to create an idea that solves the problem at hand.

REVIEWING WORK IS MORE THAN JUST THE FINAL PRESENTATION

The real secret to getting creative work approved is simple: Avoid surprises and involve the client throughout the process, not just at a presentation on the last day of the project. No one likes surprises, even good ones. A client is far more likely to buy into an idea if they feel they were involved in its creation along the way.

Avoid guessing games and chance by conducting regular reviews and being transparent about the direction in which the project is going. Take a cue from software development firms and do a 15-minute "daily stand-up" every morning where you briefly talk about what you did the previous day, and what you will do today. Most importantly, invite the client to this stand-up so they always feel involved. In addition to daily stand-ups, be sure to present work-in-progress at reviews that are scheduled no more than two weeks apart. On almost every project at Edenspiekermann, we used a "scrum" approach where work was reviewed with the client every two weeks. When you take this collaborative approach, there are no surprises and you can get it right (almost) every time.

PRESENTATION DOS AND DON'TS

RIGHT

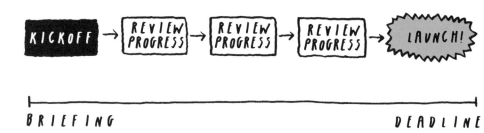

KICKOFF → REVIEW PROGRESS → REVIEW PROGRESS → REVIEW PROGRESS → LAUNCH!

BRIEFING ⊢————————————————————————————⊣ DEADLINE

WRONG

Fucked

Panic

KICKOFF ——— Silence ———→ THE BIG REVEAL --→ ?

Bad feedback

BRIEFING ⊢————————————————————————————⊣ DEADLINE

PRESENTATION BASICS
FOR NON-ASSHOLES

Even in the ideal process where the decision-makers are heavily involved in the project workflow, there are still moments when you formally present the work. Whether you are presenting the work internally to your team, to your boss, or a client, here are the fundamentals to a successful creative presentation.

PRESENT IN PERSON WHEREVER POSSIBLE

Creative work should always be presented in person or, at a bare minimum, with a phone conversation. There is no substitute for walking a client through the work, providing context and anecdotal insights as to why certain decisions were made. Sending a presentation into the abyss via an email without a proper walk-through is a recipe for disaster.

SET EXPECTATIONS PRIOR TO PRESENTING

Before the start of every presentation, make sure you clearly set expectations for what the client will see. There is nothing worse than a client interrupting a creative presentation of something like a first storyboard with, "Ahem, where are the finished animations that we were promised today?" Set expectations clearly and every presentation will go far more smoothly.

DON'T BE AFRAID TO SHOW LESS

Cut out the crap. It doesn't matter how short the presentation is; what matters is that you believe in what's in the presentation deck. If you're not sure, leave it out.

HAVE CONVICTION IN EVERYTHING YOU PRESENT

Once you have decided what will make it into your presentation deck, you need conviction in what's in there if you want to sell it to the client. Is it a single image of turd? It doesn't matter. If it shows up in the presentation, it is the greatest image of a turd in history and your client needs it. I remember a branding project at our agency where a series of internal issues meant that some absolutely awful work was produced. This came to my attention literally ten minutes before the presentation to the client. I deleted all the work from the presentation except for one slide—the moodboard (which was great). I presented this one slide to the client with conviction, explaining how this was the right direction for them. They loved it.

ALLOW JUNIORS TO PRESENT THEIR OWN WORK

At large agencies, it's commonplace for anyone short of creative director level to never interact with a client. This is a ridiculous way of working for a number of reasons. Firstly, the creative director is rarely the one doing the actual work and is probably ill-equipped to answer any detailed questions about it. Secondly, how can junior staff hope to improve their presentation skills if they do not have the opportunity to present their own work? Don't hog the spotlight. Encourage juniors to present their own work whenever possible—even in front of clients. When I worked at Edenspiekermann in Berlin, we made sure that junior staff were always client-facing. We had a simple rule: If you make it, you present it. Period.

BUILDING A GREAT PRESENTATION DECK

There is no single formula for producing a creative presentation deck. However, regardless of how you choose to display your work, the following elements should always be included.

THE PURPOSE OF THE PRESENTATION

You need a one-line description outlining the purpose of the presentation. For example, "Review the second round of logo designs based on previous feedback." Not only is it useful for the audience in the room, but it provides context when the presentation is shared with other stakeholders afterward.

WHAT YOU'LL BE SHOWING TODAY

Avoid disappointment by clearly setting expectations as to what you'll be sharing today. This is usually a simple bulleted list such as:

→ Objectives recap
→ Updated logo design sketches
→ Sample print applications
→ Sample digital applications

OBJECTIVES

Always present a recap of the objectives or goals of the project and what the creative solution will solve. Later, when you present the creative solution, you should continuously reference these goals and explain how the work addresses these needs.

THE "BIG IDEA"

What is the central idea behind the creative solution? For an ad campaign, this might be the "big idea" such as Nike's "If you have a body, you are an athlete." For a design or digital project, it might be the three guiding design or interaction principles.

THE WORK ("CREATIVE," "DESIGN," "WIREFRAMES," ETC.)

Your big moment has come—it's time to present the work itself. Each concept should be clearly labeled and have a short write-up. Where possible, show tangible examples of the work in context to illustrate how the idea will come to life. For a branding project, that may be a mock-up of the logo in context; for a digital product, a basic prototype (even just a simple click-through) is a must.

OUR RECOMMENDATION

Every creative presentation needs to have a clear recommendation as to which concept the client should choose. After all, they are paying for your expertise. If you are presenting as a team, you should be aligned beforehand on which single direction to recommend. After all, if the experts in the room cannot agree on one direction, how can you expect a client to?

RECAP

It is helpful for the client to see a recap of all the concepts side by side to act as a visual aid for discussing the work without have to click back through 137 slides.

QUESTIONS

After the recap, be sure to land on a "Questions?" slide to prompt the audience to give feedback and, unsurprisingly, to ask questions.

NEXT STEPS

Every presentation should end with a bulleted list of next steps, outlining the responsible party and the date. Everyone in the room should give verbal consensus on these next steps before the presentation ends.

ACCOUNT

ADMIN

STRATEGY

CREATIVE

LONG HOURS

When I lived in Berlin, I had an apartment in a rather fancy part of town called Prenzlauer Berg. As is very common in Berlin, there was a commercial space on the ground floor of my apartment building; in this instance, a graphic design agency. On any given weekend when I would pass by this glass-fronted floor, a team of dead-eyed creatives could be seen sitting in front of glowing iMacs. Regardless of the day, these employees toiled until the early hours of the morning. They were, like so many others, a symptom of the belief in the creative industries that you have to work long hours if you want to do great work.

Luckily for those in Germany, and most of Northern Europe, the practice of working late hours is rare, and these unlucky creatives were very much the exception. In fact, Germany and the Scandinavian countries such as Sweden and Denmark pride themselves on having some of the shortest working hours in the world[8] while producing some of the highest-quality creative work. The attitude toward long hours in these countries is: "You didn't get your work done in eight hours? You must suck at your job." Long hours are simply not celebrated.

Unfortunately, the culture in the creative industries around the rest of the world is quite different. Long hours are not only expected, they are often celebrated and even worn as a badge of pride. Working four straight weekends to meet a deadline or missing all your children's birthdays because of a pitch become legendary feats that you boast about to your coworkers. What's worst about these practices is that the brunt of long hours are done by junior or mid-level creatives who want to prove themselves and get noticed, or simply to produce great work. The reality is that working long hours does not produce better work; it does not make you a better creative or even a better human being. It just means you suck at managing your time.

SUSTAINABLE WORK IS BETTER WORK

When you work in an environment that fosters a culture of incessant long hours, neither you, the client, nor the work benefits, for a number of reasons:

→ First and foremost, the work suffers. No one does their best work when they are exhausted after spending 12 hours in front of a glowing screen. In fact, a Bureau of Labor study[9] shows that, on average, humans are productive for just under three hours per day.
→ It leads to high staff turnover. You will lose your best people (and rightly so) if you treat them like battery hens.
→ Working nonstop means that creative staff never have the space to "play." All creative people need space to reflect and work on side projects to keep them motivated, fresh, and inspired. Consistent long hours deprives them of the clear headspace when most great ideas come about.
→ You will never be able to maintain a long-term digital project that needs a consistent team for months or even years. When I worked in Berlin, we spent almost four years on the development of one (of many) major digital platforms for Red Bull. There is simply no way you could have run a project like that if the team were expected to work at 110% for this period of time. Ad agency folks in particular should take note of this one.
→ Overtime hours worked by creatives are rarely billed to clients, so the value of the design work is greatly diminished.

[8] http://www.bbc.com/news/business-34677949
[9] https://www.inc.com/melanie-curtin/in-an-8-hour-day-the-average-worker-is-productive-for-this-many-hours.html

AM I OVERWORKED?

1. Place <u>one</u> X on any day that you worked more than eight hours

2. Place <u>two</u> Xs for any weekend days that you worked

M O N T H						
M	T	W	T	F	S	S

RESULTS:

0–5 Normal
5–10 Overworked
10+ Get the fuck out of there

HOW TO CREATE A SUSTAINABLE WORK ENVIRONMENT

I hear you—saying "don't work long hours" is fine in theory. Applying it in the real world, with clients, deadlines, competition, and, above all, a drive for creative excellence is a different matter entirely. However, believe me, it can be done. All over Northern Europe there are thousands of creatives who will leave their studio, agency, or workplace before 6pm. With some basic process optimizations in your workflow, anyone can create a sustainable work environment without sacrificing great work and still keep clients happy. It starts with some basics.

INVOLVE ALL CORE COMPETENCES WHEN SCOPING A PROJECT

Long hours occur because there is too much work to do in too little time. Much of the time this happens due to poor project scoping. Always take the time to properly scope a project from the start and, most importantly, involve all the key competences in your team—not just the account manager and the creative director. Including representation from all facets of a project, from developers to copywriters, means that the timeline and workload will be grounded in reality rather than the account director's idea of what the client wants to hear (see the "Scoping" chapter for more details on this).

BE TRANSPARENT WITH THE CLIENT WHEN THINGS GO WRONG

Whether it's with your client or your own boss, be transparent at all times. If something goes wrong that will affect the timeline, don't sweep it under the rug and hope for the best. "Hoping for the best" usually results in weeks of long hours at the end of a project. Instead of trying to cram in an unreasonable amount of work (which will certainly affect the quality), discuss it with the client immediately. In most cases, a compromised solution can be found that achieves the same goal. This is common in building digital products where a certain feature—for example, a video player—takes longer to build than originally expected due to technical complexity. Instead of trying to cram everything in, ask the client if there is some complexity that can be reduced in order to deliver it on time. In the case of the video player, perhaps they don't need the "save to playlist" version for the first release? Having these discussions in a timely fashion keeps everyone on the same page and avoids nasty surprises, long hours, and rushed work.

> ANYONE CAN CREATE A SUSTAINABLE WORK ENVIRONMENT WITHOUT SACRIFICING GREAT WORK

CREATIVE PROJECTS WILL ALWAYS FILL AVAILABLE TIME

Scenario A:

HOURS WORKED

AVAILABLE TIME

Scenario B:

H O U R S   W O R K E D

AVAILABLE TIME

DON'T BE AFRAID TO SAY NO

Creatives (myself included) want to push their work (and themselves) to the limit and therefore rarely say no to any request. This can be balanced by a good senior leader or account person who can push back on unreasonable client requests. Unfortunately, outside of the Northern European countries, account directors all too often take the side of the client, and the word "no" seems to be missing from their vocabulary. These types of sales-focused individuals have no place in managing creative projects and should be replaced.

SALES-FOCUSED INDIVIDUALS HAVE NO PLACE IN MANAGING CREATIVE PROJECTS

ALWAYS TIMEBOX TASKS, ESPECIALLY FOR JUNIOR STAFF

Creatives, especially juniors, will fill whatever time is available with work. They are also eager to prove themselves and their work. For these reasons, it is important to manage their time for them, and give them very clear goals and deadlines to present work. If you are a creative leader, always make sure junior staff leave the office before you do.

PROCESS. PROCESS. PROCESS.

To creatives, "process" may sound like a dirty word, but in truth, initiating process in a creative workplace is key to a sustainable environment. From simple optimizations such as increasing meeting efficiency through basic meeting etiquette, to introducing a standardized process for dealing with unwieldy client requests, having commonly understood processes across your workplace reduces wasted time, and therefore increases the likelihood of everyone being able to go home on time.

SUSTAINABLE WORKING USING AGILE METHODOLOGY

One of the ways in which we achieved a sustainable working environment at Edenspiekermann was by introducing Agile working methodology for almost all of our projects. "Agile" is an iterative approach to producing digital products in a timeboxed, incremental fashion, instead of trying to deliver it all at once near the end[10]. This methodology was developed in the 1980s for software development, but its usage has now spread far beyond software companies and technology. Many forward-looking design agencies and teams utilize it to create sustainable working processes for their projects. At Edenspiekermann, we used Agile systems to ensure sustainable work practices for everything from building digital products to brand design and campaigns.

The Agile setup breaks down projects into small features called user stories, prioritizes them, and then delivers them continuously in two-week cycles called "sprints." At the end of each sprint, the respective piece of work is reviewed by the "product owner" and either released or revised.

The Agile team always works as one team, is never siloed into competences, and is flat in leadership. Agile is geared toward sustainable long-term work and is perfect for any creative or technology project that runs for four weeks or more. Smaller projects will generally not work in an

[10] http://www.agilenutshell.com

THE AGILE PROCESS

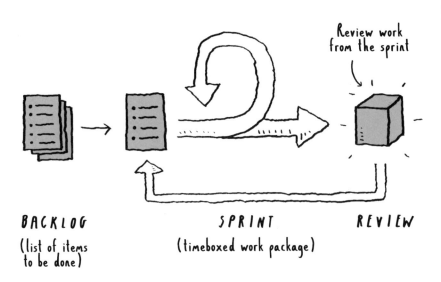

Review work
from the sprint

BACKLOG
(list of items
to be done)

SPRINT
(timeboxed work package)

REVIEW

Agile setup, as the layer of processes or rituals required outweighs the benefits and efficiencies gained over a long period of time.

THE ROLES IN AN AGILE PROJECT

The product owner
This is the decision-maker and guardian of the product vision. In a client-agency relationship, there are usually two product owners: one client-side, and one agency-side.

The team
The people doing the work. Most importantly, they are an interdisciplinary group working side by side as a single team—designers, developers, and writers, depending on the needs of the project. They are autonomous, flat in hierarchy, and empowered to make their own decisions. Often (in the best cases) they are a mix of agency and client-side individuals working as one team.

The scrum master

The scrum master is not part of the team and does not influence decisions. Rather, they facilitate the process and help remove blocks that prevent the team from working. In an agency-client relationship, they often handle the administration side of the client relationship.

When an Agile process is used in an agency environment, the client is integrated into the team from the start in the role of a product owner. They are involved in the planning of timeboxed sprints. At the start of each sprint, together with the design/technology team, they plan a list of features (known as "user stories") that will be completed in that sprint, and the team estimates the amount of effort required to complete these tasks. A scrum master (the facilitator of the process) informs the team and the product owner how many working days are in the sprint (considering budget and availability of staff members). Based on this number, the team commits to a set number of features. For example, if the team has 20 working days in the sprint, and the estimate to complete the selected tasks is 30 days, then the product owner must remove some tasks before the team commits. It's simple math.

TRANSPARENCY AND TRUST ARE PARAMOUNT FOR AN AGILE PROCESS TO WORK

Transparency and trust are paramount for an Agile process to work. The commitment between the team and the product owner at each sprint planning becomes almost sacred: The product owner agrees not to push extra work into the sprint, and the team agrees to deliver the work to which they committed. There is almost always a degree of struggle to convince a client to adopt an Agile process for their project, but when they do, they (and your team) will thank you for it.

QUIZ

HOW SHOULD YOU REWARD YOUR TEAM FOR WORKING LATE?

(A)

BEER FRIDGE

(B)

COOL OFFICE SHIT

(C)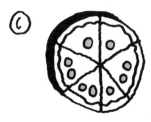

FREE PIZZA

(D)

A LOVELY CAKE

(E)

COMP DAYS

(F)

HEARTY THANKS

ANSWER: E

WHAT HAPPENS WHEN I DO NEED MY TEAM TO WORK LATE?

Of course, sometimes there's an important design proposal to finish, or it's the week before a major project launch and long hours are inevitable. Let's be clear—there is nothing wrong with working late occasionally. However, if you are a creative leader, it is still paramount to respect people's personal time. If you need your team to work late, be sure to do the following.

GIVE ADVANCE NOTICE AND ASK YOUR TEAM FIRST

If you have a deadline, proposal, or something else that mandates late working, ask your staff first and, most importantly, in advance. Working late should never be mandatory—it should genuinely be optional. It's amazing how far a simple "Hey guys, sorry to ask, but would you mind working a couple of hours extra tonight?" will go.

COVER LATE FOOD AND TRAVEL COSTS

In our office, we have a rule that if people work after 7pm they get dinner provided. If they work after 8pm the company will pay for them to get a cab home. These are the bare minimum to offer your team for working late. However, covering these expenses should not be treated as compensation for working late, but rather a minimum comfort level for invading someone's personal time.

ENFORCE COMP DAYS

While buying your creative team pizza, beers, and a cab home is great, when someone works late you offer them time in lieu. Not at some vague point in the future "when we're less busy," but at a concrete time—for example, the next day or extending their upcoming weekend.

GET YOUR HANDS DIRTY TOO

Are you an art director? Even a creative overlord? Consider tech companies and their flat hierarchies. The best creative directors I have worked with have earned respect for being hands-on. Need your team to work late for a pitch or a deadline? Stay late and do some work too.

REMEMBER: IT IS JUST A FUCKING JOB

As enjoyable and rewarding as a career in the creative industries can be, it is just a job, and it is simply not worth sacrificing your family, friends, or health for. Every time you are going to work a late night that means you'll miss a family dinner or a kid's birthday, ask yourself: "Is it worth it?" If you have to ask yourself that question more than once a month, chances are it isn't.

I'll never forget an article by the late Saatchi & Saatchi and BBDO ad-man Linds Redding. In a poignant 3000-word essay[11], the creative director—terminally ill with esophageal cancer at the time—reflected on a career in the ad industry and the resulting long hours, missed birthdays, and anniversaries. It culminated in this sentiment: "So was it worth it? Well, of course not. It turns out it was just advertising. There was no higher calling. No ultimate prize." Keep these words in mind whenever you think about missing your kid's birthday for a deadline.

ASK YOURSELF: "IS IT WORTH IT?" IF YOU HAVE TO ASK YOURSELF THAT QUESTION MORE THAN ONCE A MONTH, CHANCES ARE IT ISN'T.

[11] http://www.thesfegotist.com/editorial/2012/march/14/short-lesson-perspective

CLIENTS

Cast your mind back to the poster I mentioned at the very beginning of this book: "Don't work with assholes. Don't work for assholes." Now, while we might all agree on this sentiment in principle (after all, you probably wouldn't still be reading this book if you didn't), the reality of the creative industries is that they are commercial operations centered around making money. What happens when the asshole is the person paying you a lot of money, keeping the lights of the agency on, and making sure you and your creatives are employed?

Enforcing a client "no-asshole" policy is certainly trickier than enforcing one with yourself or with your team. Except in the case of the most famous and sought-after creatives, a "take it or leave it" attitude is not really a viable way to deal with difficult clients. Now, although there certainly is the rare asshole client, it is my opinion that a productive partnership is possible with the vast majority of clients—even the difficult ones—once they are managed, and understood, correctly.

THE TRUTH ABOUT CLIENTS

The friction between creatives and clients is almost legendary. Even beyond the creative industries, popular culture is filled with humorous tales of the seemingly endless battles between flustered creatives and clueless clients. Indeed, so numerous are these tales that the writer David Thorne[12] has made an entire career out of this cat-and-mouse game, writing book after book filled with hilarious semi-fictional anecdotes about the interactions between egoistic creatives and witless clients who always seem to want more and more for less and less money.

Despite what some creatives may tell you, the vast majority of clients are not assholes. In fact, most are nice, sensible humans who just want to do a good job, impress their boss, and get recognition for the work they do. They are not out to destroy "great work." They are not out to screw up our weekends or crush our dreams. They just want to get good results, on time and on budget, and not get fired. Many client and creative relationship issues come down to egoistic creatives, who forget that the client also has a job to do and a boss to please. When a client hires a creative or an agency, they put their neck on the line by placing their trust in a third party to deliver for them. Regardless of how innovative the work is or how many awards it wins, it is not worth risking their job for if it is not delivered on time or on budget.

Remember, the number-one rule: Design is not art. You are not Picasso. You are not even George W. Bush painting in his basement. You are working for a commercial practice that has stakeholders, budgets, bosses, and deadlines. Keep this ingrained in your psyche for every client engagement and you probably won't go too far wrong.

TRADITIONAL CLIENT MANAGEMENT

Those who have worked in more traditional agencies are undoubtedly familiar with the "layered" approach to managing a client relationship. By this I mean an organization structure that is more complex than a government agency. When I first worked in a big agency, I was amazed by the sheer number of roles needed to manage a client. A typical mid-sized project at a large agency could have this many layers, with only the top few levels allowed to interact with the client:

[12]http://www.27bslash6.com

ORDER OF PRIORITIES

CLIENT	CREATIVE
1. ON BUDGET	1. WIN AWARDS
2. ON DEADLINE	2. BE FAMOUS
3. IMPRESS BOSS	3. IMPRESS PEERS
4. ON-BRAND	4. IMPRESS BOSS
5. IMPRESS PEERS	5. ON-BRAND
6. WIN AWARDS	6. ON-DEADLINE
7. BE FAMOUS	7. ON-BUDGET
8. CREATIVE IS HAPPY	8. CLIENT IS HAPPY

→ Account director*
→ Project manager
→ Senior planner*
→ Planner
→ Group creative director*
→ Creative director
→ Associate creative director
→ Art director
→ Copywriter
→ Senior developer
→ Developer
→ Designer
→ Junior designer
→ Production designer

* = "worthy" of interaction with a client

It is my belief that this approach doesn't work, especially for digital projects. In an era where design and technology need to work closely together, things move faster and projects are longer and more complex than ever. Collaboration on complex technical topics simply cannot be mediated via layers of intermediaries. The tech guy in the agency needs to be able to pick up the phone and talk to the tech guy on the client side directly without five people in between. Compare the layered "agency cake" to how teams at tech companies operate. Their teams are autonomous, efficient, flat in hierarchy, and employing smart generalists who can manage themselves, their work, and others. Agencies can definitely learn from this when it comes to managing client relationships.

THE SECRET TO LASTING CLIENT RELATIONSHIPS

I am not a believer in schmoozing clients. Quite frankly, I am terrible at it. I've worked with many creative directors and account directors who are masters of small talk over fancy lunches. Much of this behavior is sales bullshit, and I have no time for it. My personal approach to successfully working with clients long term is simple: I am the person they know they can trust to deliver great work and I will not let them down. They need honesty, transparency, and great work, not someone to be their friend.

BE HONEST, EVEN IF IT IS UNPOPULAR

Honesty and transparency are the most important parts of building any client relationship. If the client doesn't trust you, there is no point in doing anything together. All too often, creative agencies stretch the truth and overpromise in the name of winning projects. Omitting the truth for financial gain is also commonplace in agencies. They might fail to disclose that they are outsourcing the entire development to a third-party company in Colombia. They might not tell an inexperienced client that they could do this project better with a freelancer instead of an agency. They might know that a specific project is bad for the client's business but take it on anyway to make a quick buck. It is better to be honest and lose a project now in order to build trust for something bigger in the future.

MAKE THE CLIENT PART OF THE TEAM

Creating divisions between client and agency personnel simply doesn't work. The more you divide up, the more the "us and them" mentality seeps in. In addition, despite what traditional agency people would lead you to believe, a collaborative approach to creating work is far more effective than keeping the agency in its own bubble. Change the approach from a mindset of "the client and the agency" to a mindset of "one project team" and reap the benefits. After all, while the agency may be the experts in the field of design, advertising, or technology, the client knows their business best. Leverage that knowledge by involving the client in all stages of the process, including co-creation and brainstorming sessions.

HONESTY AND TRANSPARENCY ARE THE MOST IMPORTANT PARTS OF BUILDING ANY CLIENT RELATIONSHIP.

The best example I can give for this comes from a few years ago, when the Dutch office of our agency was developing a new service to improve speed and safety at train platforms in the Netherlands. The idea was to create a cutting-edge digital display running the length of the platform which would indicate which train cars were empty in advance of the train arriving at the platform (so people could line up in the optimal part of the platform before the train arrived). The big question was, how could we figure out which train cars were full? Would we need to install some costly cutting-edge tech? During a co-creation session with the clients, the stakeholder, and the agency, the group was struggling with how we could figure out whether the train car was full or whether this idea was doomed to fail. Then, a member of the railway team announced that there were already infrared sensors on the train that could be used. This unexpected insight from a member of the client's team single-handedly shaped the entire direction of the project.

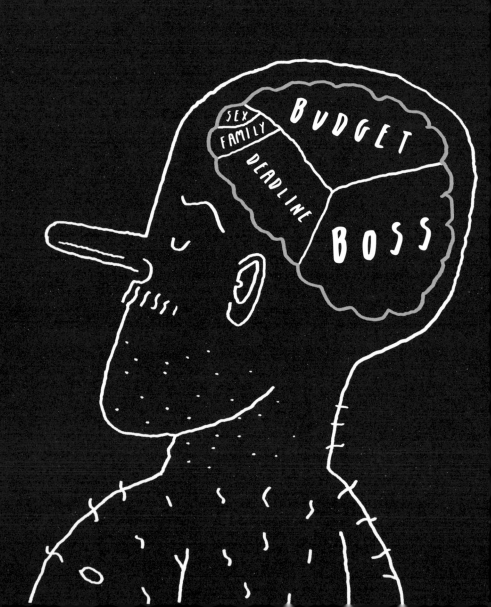

SHARE PROGRESS WORK REGULARLY
Traditionally, agencies worked with a client much like a service provider. The agency or creative team would receive the project brief and then disappear until the deadline. They would eventually emerge with a piece of work that the client would not see until the day of the presentation. Instead of a "big reveal" approach like this, build trust with your client by involving them in the process with regular reviews and updates.

DON'T SUGARCOAT THE BAD NEWS
Once a project is up and running, there will no doubt be a moment (every project has at least one) when there is bad news to tell the client. Don't let it fester and resist the urge to cover it up. Immediately and calmly flag the problem with your suggested solution. Transparency wins every time.

PLAY WELL WITH IN-HOUSE TEAMS
Given the growth—and indeed the quality—of in-house design teams, integrating with these teams is critical. Don't be a dick. In a lot of cases, these teams outstrip agencies in terms of talent and skill. In my experience at Edenspiekermann, some of our most fruitful partnerships (and best work) have come about when there is little or no divide between us and the client-side design team. We work in the same space, brainstorm together, and split the workload between ourselves.

DIFFICULT CLIENTS

Despite the best intentions, some clients are simply difficult to work with. It may come down to a lack of experience, them having a difficult boss themselves, insecurity in their position, or a multitude of other things. Nonetheless, in most cases, great work and a good partnership are possible with even the most difficult of clients.

In my experience, there are several archetypes of difficult clients.

THE NOVICE
Whether it's their first time commissioning an agency, or they're just new to the job, an inexperienced client, no matter how well-meaning, can present particular challenges for an agency. A junior client can often need a more seasoned hand from the agency than a senior client. Given their lack of experience in their company, they can often be Yes Men (or Women) who are well-intentioned but not confident enough to push back when they

get feedback from the tiers above. Producing truly excellent work with novice clients is difficult as they will rarely take risks. They require a firm but patient hand. As an agency, our role with these types of clients is not only to complete the project, but also to guide, mentor, and provide a positive experience for them.

THE HIGH DEMANDER

This type of client is often a little neurotic, needing constant reassurance and project updates. In many cases, this may stem from personal insecurity and a need to micromanage. My advice for this type of client is to create full transparency at every stage of the project and make them feel safe. A Kanban-style workflow organization board such as Trello or Jira can help, as they can see the process of individual tasks over the course of the week. However, it is critical with this type of client that you properly shield your working team from their feedback. If you don't, nothing will get done.

THE WANNABE CREATIVE

The wannabe creative is an irritating but harmless type of client. They could be an ex-agency person, or even an in-house designer at the client's company who has found their way onto the board of stakeholders as the internal voice of design. These individuals are often jealous of the "cool agency" coming in, and if not correctly managed can sabotage your ideas. My advice for these types of individuals is to involve them as much as possible and make them feel valued. Invite them to work together in your office. Involve them in brainstorms. The real trick with the wannabe creative is to make them think they came up with your idea themselves. This turns them into a powerful ally who can act as an internal force in selling your ideas.

ASSHOLE CLIENTS

True assholes are rare, but usually there is an underlying reason for clients being difficult. Perhaps they have been burned by an agency before, or their own work environment sucks. The best solution is to try to find out what issues or politics are at play and then make their life as easy as possible. This might involve factoring in an extra presentation for their boss, or providing them with useful insights to help them do their job. Try to make them look good and you won't go far wrong.

If a client is truly an asshole, in that they abuse or demean agency staff in a personal manner, there is only one solution: Tell them to go fuck themselves.

10 TIPS FOR CLIENTS TO GET THE BEST FROM YOUR CREATIVES

1. Give good briefings.

2. Clearly convey budget/timeline restrictions <u>beforehand</u>.

3. Don't micromanage.

4. Always reward the team for pushing for new ideas (even if you don't use them).

5. Give clear, constructive feedback.

6. Listen—remember, you have hired a professional to do something you cannot.

7. Be organized—there's only so much a creative team can do if you are a mess.

8. Be available.

9. Be interested and involved.

10. Share your partner's business insights— not their opinions on the color of the logo.

HIRING & BEING HIRED

Great work is made, unsurprisingly, by great people. It follows that if you hire B-list people, you'll get B-list work. It's a no-brainer. Attracting great people is hard. Keeping them is even harder. However, all too often agencies make crucial mistakes in the rush to hire great people.

Now, let's assume a creative business has a great reputation. You do great work. You pay well and have a good work/life balance. Your culture is surprisingly free of egomaniacs. Unfortunately, however, even the most well-meaning creative business can fall short when it comes to basic hiring etiquette. Creative businesses—especially smaller ones—are notoriously bad when it comes to dealing with key aspects of hiring. Forgetting simple steps, such as not replying to incoming correspondence that isn't immediately of value, frequently tarnishes the reputations of what are otherwise great creative businesses. For example, an HR department will jump through all the hoops when they need someone with your exact skills, but what happens if you're a junior with no experience, an intern, or just someone who doesn't currently fit their profile? The chances of getting a reply are slim. Remember, the measure of how you treat people is how you treat them when you don't need something from them.

It is beyond the scope of this book to provide you, dear reader, with an exhaustive guide to finding great creative talent or indeed finding a great job yourself—you have the wonderful world of the internet for that. However, when it comes to attracting, hiring, and keeping great talent, there are a number of key points to keep in mind.

BASIC JOB APPLICATION ETIQUETTE

An agency can do great work, pay well, have a good work/life balance and an ego-free culture, but all of that means jack shit if it fails to properly handle incoming correspondence from enthusiastic young creatives or intern applications. Even the best-intending agencies fall down when it comes to replying and this is generally chalked up to: "We were slammed. We run a business, after all. Clients come first!" My friend, the creative world is a small one and this will come to bite you on the ass sooner or later.

We've all been there. You do an interview. It seems to go well and the potential employer tells you that they will contact you in a couple of days. You go home feeling good. A week passes. Silence. You send a polite follow-up email. Nothing. Another week passes. Cue tumbleweed. A phone call. Zilch. How hard is it to get a reply? Now, a side note to young design graduates applying for a job: Do not expect people to reply immediately. Do not even expect them to reply any time soon. Do not hassle them. Do not be an annoying little shit. But do expect an answer eventually. You took the time to write to a creative director, design director, HR department, etc. and you do deserve a response. Sure, it might take a while—agency people are always busy—but they owe you an answer.

EVEN THE MOST WELL-MEANING CREATIVE BUSINESS CAN FALL SHORT WHEN IT COMES TO BASIC HIRING ETIQUETTE.

Like every other creative, I have my first-hand story on this topic. After graduating university, I set about finding my first internship. I researched every design company in Ireland, eventually shortlisting about 20 agencies that matched my skillset. I created an Excel spreadsheet detailing each agency's history, address, staff, clients, projects, awards, star signs, favorite underwear color—the list went on. It was an obsessively detailed piece of research that would make even the most diligent accountant proud. Once I had my list, I prepared an individual letter and a different portfolio for each of the agencies on my list. After almost four weeks of full-time work on this assignment, I finally sent the letters and portfolios to the chosen agencies.

HOW NOT TO SCREW UP YOUR NEXT INTERVIEW

Brush hair, you're not an artist

Prepare three smart questions

Research into who you're meeting

No disgusting food stains

Bring five copies of your resumé

Bring five examples of your best work

Bring a notebook

Don't act like you know more font names than the creative director

Wear shoes that don't make you look like either a hipster or a homeless person

After a few weeks of not hearing anything back, I followed up with a gentle reminder. Nothing. After two months of silence, I decided that if I was going to be rejected, I wanted to be rejected by the best people in the business, not a small-time agency in Ireland. I decided to leave Ireland, never to return. That day I promised myself that, when I ran my own agency, I would make a point to reply to every piece of correspondence, no matter how long it took. I'm proud to say that I have kept that promise to this day (admittedly, sometimes my replies take a long time).

Two days after writing to Edenspiekermann Berlin, one of the most prestigious agencies in Europe, they responded to offer me an interview. It gave me a real tickle a few years later when one of the agencies that had ignored me sent a highly flattering email attempting to court me into joining their company. At this stage, I had worked my way up to become design director at Edenspiekermann Berlin. They were looking for a head of digital to save their sinking graphic-design business. Of course, they had no idea that they had ignored email after email several years previously when I was offering to make their tea in exchange for a few hours of unpaid work experience. The exchange looked something like this (opposite). I may have modified this narrative for dramatic effect ...

I DECIDED THAT IF I WAS GOING TO BE REJECTED, I WANTED TO BE REJECTED BY THE BEST PEOPLE IN THE BUSINESS

Remember, no matter how successful, busy, or famous you are, you should always reply to applications and interview requests. There is no excuse for being a dick—and karma can be a bitch.

NEGOTIATING SALARIES

Creative people are often terrible at negotiating. We are driven by interesting projects and the opportunity to work with great people in a cool environment. The very best people are never driven by money alone. This is even more true of young talent who are looking to get started in the industry and build their portfolio. Therefore, it is easy for an unscrupulous agency to take advantage of junior creatives, especially at the salary negotiation stage. It is all too common for the hiring agency to lowball the salary offer in the promise of "great portfolio opportunities," "exciting brands," or, the most patronizing of all, "a chance to work with the best people in the business." Bullshit. If you are being offered a job, regardless of your experience level, you are a professional and deserve to be paid like one.

Hi Paul,

Hope things are going well at Edenspiekermann. Currently we're looking for a new head of digital and we'd love to talk to you about the role. We think you'd be a great fit here at Pricks-R-Us.

Of course, don't worry about the fact we ignored all your emails before you went and worked at a famous agency in Berlin. We think you're great now and well worthy of this shameless suck-up email. No hard feelings, you know how it is—busy with clients, etc., etc. All good now old chum.

Let me know if this might interest you.

Best,

Patrick Prickleworth

Dear Mr. Prickleworth,

Thank you for your email. Things are indeed going well at Edenspiekermann Berlin and I have no intention of moving any time soon.

I hope your company continues to fail, you contract an incurable form of leprosy, and your coastal office sinks into the ocean.

Yours sincerely,

Paul

INTERVIEW RED FLAGS

- [ ] Evidence of long hours.

- [ ] People eating lunch at their desks.

- [ ] Excessive office comforts that indicate staff are encouraged to work longer.

- [ ] Lack of diversity in interview panel.

- [ ] Lack of visible diverse leadership.

- [ ] Creative leadership and creative teams sit separately.

- [ ] Any sort of nonsense jibberish like "It's all about the work here."

- [ ] A creative director who has their own face printed on a T-shirt or cup.

More than two boxes checked? Stay away.

GOOD OFFER/BAD OFFER?

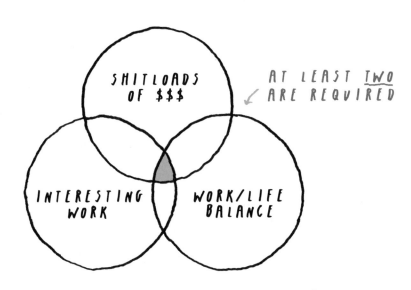

It's not only junior staff who get taken advantage of when it comes to salary negotiations. Foreign workers on employer-sponsored work visas are especially vulnerable to unscrupulous practices. When an expat is relying on an employer-sponsored work visa, that employer can easily take advantage of the situation on two fronts. Firstly, they can offer a "take it or leave it" attitude by leveraging the work visa as the "only way in" carrot. Secondly, they can plead ignorance of local currency differences. A starting salary of $50,000 might seem like a small fortune to a creative director coming from certain parts of the world, but in actual fact they should be earning well over $100,000. Both are disgusting practices and I encourage you, dear reader, to name and shame any agencies who partake in them.

When I first came to the US, I was very lucky to work with HUGE, an agency with a great HR department who always pay and treat expats very fairly. Unfortunately, not all creative agencies are like this. Cheap labor doesn't just happen in the construction industry. I've heard that quite a few expats working in creative agencies in the US are paid much less than the American employees.

The bottom line: If you are in a hiring role, don't mess around with people who are in a vulnerable position. Offer a fair salary from the start. In the infamous words of Mike Monteiro, legendary co-founder and design director of Mule Design, "Fuck you, pay me." [13] Mark my words, it is very easy to get a reputation for taking advantage of vulnerable staff. It will spread around the industry like wildfire and, once it takes hold, it is very difficult to shake.

PAY YOUR INTERNS

It goes without saying that you should pay your interns. They are not a source of free labor. They are not there just to make your tea. It is, of course, totally acceptable for interns to bear the brunt of production work, mounting, art supply store runs, etc., but that doesn't mean they shouldn't be paid. Despite their inexperience, interns bring curiosity, a wonderfully naive fresh eye, and energy to any agency that no seasoned professional can contribute. All the best agencies have some sort of intern or trainee program, as fresh students transform an agency environment for the better. Often, interns are more skilled in the latest trends and tricks than senior staff. If you can't afford to pay them, don't hire them.

> **DESPITE THEIR INEXPERIENCE, INTERNS BRING CURIOSITY, A WONDERFULLY NAIVE FRESH EYE, AND ENERGY**

[13] https://www.youtube.com/watch?v=jVkLVRt6c1U

INTERN ETIQUETTE

SHOULD

**BE GIVEN TASKS
THEY CAN LEARN FROM**

BE GIVEN A MENTOR

BE PAID

SHOULD *NOT*

**BE STUCK DOING
MINDLESS TASKS**

**BE FORCED TO WORK
LONG HOURS**

**BE EXPECTED TO
MAKE YOUR TEA**

LEAVING & FIRING

The world of the creative industries is very small. No matter how you part ways with someone, you will inevitably encounter them again. The industry has a way of dealing you back people you would much rather have forgotten later in your career, except this time they have superpowers. It's like encountering Bowser in a game of Super Mario Brothers—every time you think he's gone, he makes a surprise return, except now he can throw fireballs. The person you fire today may very well be your boss or your client in the future.

Here's a personal example of how serendipity works in this industry: In 2016 I was hired as CCO of Edenspiekermann, who I had worked for previously in Berlin but quit in order to move to a new job in New York. Had I been a dick when I left Edenspiekermann, I certainly wouldn't have been asked back to be their CCO. The ex-boss at my first design agency internship in Dublin wrote the reference letter that got me the work visa for my first job in the US. Had I been a dick when I resigned from that internship, I wouldn't have got that useful recommendation letter, nor would I have got that visa.

The small world doesn't end with agencies. With more and more creatives moving to in-house roles, the flow of people between agency and in-house jobs is more fluid than ever. For example, an ex-employee I worked with in New York is now the design director at a big tech company. An ex-intern at Edenspiekermann Berlin became a major client of the Los Angeles office. He commissioned the agency because of the great experience he had had as an intern. The list goes on. Think of every professional relationship as something that never truly ends, but will resurface again in another form until one of you either dies or retires. In other words, what goes around, comes around.

PARTING WAYS IS HARD

Whether you are resigning from a job or letting someone go, it is always difficult. There can be a feeling of betrayal among your team. Mix into that the volatile nature of creative people (the best creatives are always the most

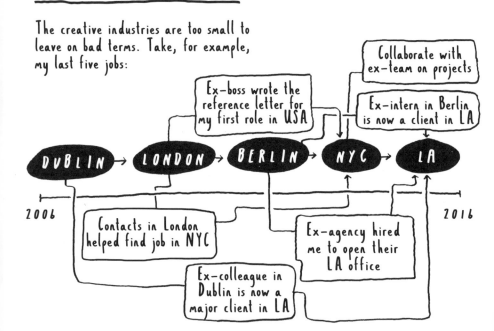

IT'S A SMALL WORLD ...

The creative industries are too small to leave on bad terms. Take, for example, my last five jobs:

Collaborate with ex-team on projects

Ex-boss wrote the reference letter for my first role in USA

Ex-intern in Berlin is now a client in LA

DUBLIN → LONDON → BERLIN → NYC → LA

2006   2016

Contacts in London helped find job in NYC

Ex-agency hired me to open their LA office

Ex-colleague in Dublin is now a major client in LA

unstable) and there's bound to be some disappointment—or indeed drama. Several years ago, I experienced this in person when I was leaving my agency job to move cities.

An old colleague of mine from when I worked in Europe—let's call him Tommy Togglesmith—was one of the most talented individuals I've ever worked with. Over the years, we worked on dozens of projects together, from rebranding toilet paper to branding apps. In fact, some of the best work I've created was done in collaboration with him. Almost every evening, at 6pm on the dot, we would crack open a beer at our desks and discuss whatever project roadblock or insane client request was the topic of the day. We worked countless late nights together under the most ridiculous deadlines. So when the time came for me to leave the agency, I knew it was not going to be easy.

It was a rainy Friday afternoon in our favorite bar when I broke the news: I was leaving the company for a new job. Tommy fixed me with a strange look that I have never seen before or since. He closed his eyes and stood perfectly still. Even though we were in the middle of a relatively busy bar, everything seemed to pause. It was like a scene in *The Matrix* when everything freezes except for the hero and the villain in midair. Suddenly, Tommy turned to me and let out a bloodcurdling, "Fuuuuuuuuuuuuuuuuuuuuck!", "Fuuuuck!" and finally, "Fuuuuuuuuuuuuuuuuuuuuuuuuuu uuuuuuuuuuuuck!" and promptly walked out of the bar. I genuinely thought he was going to return to bludgeon me to a bloody pulp with his bare hands. We laugh about it now, but leaving your creative is like breaking up with an ex. It is bloody tough.

THINK OF EVERY PROFESSIONAL RELATIONSHIP AS SOMETHING THAT NEVER TRULY ENDS, BUT WILL RESURFACE AGAIN IN ANOTHER FORM

Anyone who has worked with a great team of creatives understands the close bonds that you form. You are brothers-in-arms, facing the madness of agency life. You stand together against insane deadlines, neurotic clients, and egomaniac creative directors. You savor the highs of successfully selling in that great idea together. You mourn the idea that was killed by an overzealous legal team together. You spend more hours with them than your partner or kids. Your creative team is your family away from home. Parting ways with them—no matter how innocent the reasons—is hard. But there are certainly ways to improve the handling of these situations.

SHOULD I FIRE SOMEONE?

Start here →

WHAT IS THE REASON?

NOT PRODUCING GREAT WORK

TIME MANAGEMENT ISSUES

FINANCIAL REASONS (e.g. downsizing)

UNFORGIVABLE OFFENCE (e.g. murdering the office dog)

DID THEY IMPROVE WITH FEEDBACK?

YES   NO

DID THEY IMPROVE WITH FEEDBACK?

YES   NO

ARE THEY A CULTURAL FIT?

YES   NO

KEEP THEM

Good people that are a cultural fit are hard to find. Give opportunity to improve or try to find an alternative role for them.

LET THEM GO

But don't be an asshole about it. Offer a severance package and a fair notice period (four weeks is fair).

IMMEDIATE FIRE

Get lost. Pack your stuff and say Auf Wiedersehen. Your time here is up, asshole.

How To Leave A Job Without Being An Asshole

So you've decided to leave your job. You've had enough of the egomaniac traits of the creative director who insists on you working every weekend. Maybe you want to start your own agency. Or maybe you and your family are moving across the country and it isn't possible to continue. No matter what the reason, always leave a role in a professional and amicable manner.

OFFER CONTINUED SUPPORT TO YOUR OLD TEAM
At Edenspiekermann Berlin, I offered (and followed through on) continued support to my old team to provide any guidance and answer questions for a few weeks while they transitioned to a new team leader. Even though I had already started my new job, I knew I was responsible for a smooth handover.

GIVE AMPLE NOTICE, NO MATTER WHAT THE OFFICIAL NOTICE PERIOD IS
This might sound obvious, but it is surprising how often creatives don't do this. If you are in any way good at your job, people depend on you. I gave eight weeks' notice at one job. However, employers please take note: For this to work, you need to create an environment where people feel valued.

SEND A PERSONAL THANK YOU NOTE TO EVERYONE
And before you ask, yes, even send one to the egomaniac creative director. Take the high road and give praise and thank him or her for their mentorship.

ALWAYS SPEAK HIGHLY OF YOUR OLD ROLE
I regularly include positive anecdotes from my previous jobs in articles and on social media (despite the fact that they are technically my competition now that I run another agency). This applies even if you hated your old job.

When it comes to a positive transition when a staff member leaves, the employer also has a role to play. Sometimes, your staff outgrow you. Creative people need to move around and gain different experiences in order to thrive. I think the average lifecycle of a junior to mid-level creative at an agency should be no more than three years. In fact, I would strongly recommend to any junior creative not to stay at any one agency for more than three years, no matter how difficult it may be for the agency to handle their loss. At the start of their career, creatives can only learn so much at one place, then they need to try something different. Regardless of how difficult it may be, as an employer and a mentor you should never show your disappointment when a creative tells you they are leaving. Instead, thank them for their services and wish them all the best.

FIRING

Letting people go is part of running any business, and there is nothing wrong with firing someone if it is handled correctly. Never feel guilty or hesitate about firing someone if it is for the right reasons. A creative workplace is first and foremost a business, and that comes first. However, there's no need to be an asshole about it either.

Being let go, regardless of the reason, is humiliating for anyone. On top of that, creative people have a more sensitive disposition than most—they are easily crushed. Generally speaking, a measured dose of constructive feedback can be useful. Be sure to thank them for their services. Highlight their good traits and, if appropriate, suggest what you feel would be a good next step in their career. Unless they have murdered the office dog, offer a reference letter, a reasonable notice period and, if appropriate, a severance package. Before you let someone go, you should do the following.

GIVE CLEAR ROOM FOR IMPROVEMENT
If the person is a great cultural fit for your team, and you genuinely think there is a chance for improvement, provide this opportunity with clear, achievable goals within a 30-day timebox. These goals should give them an opportunity to work on the weaknesses that led you to consider firing them. For example, if a creative is failing to deliver work on time, then demonstrating improved timekeeping skills would be the focus of the 30-day probation.

IS THERE ANOTHER ROLE THEY COULD FILL?
If the individual is a great personality addition to the office and a hard worker, before you let them go, ask yourself if there is another role they could fill. I've seen this happen a few times quite successfully. A few years ago we hired a visual designer who, while terrible at visual design, turned out to be a great strategist. I know a copywriter who wasn't great at writing ads but was given the opportunity to work on the editorial team, where they excelled.

FIRING SOMEONE WITHOUT BEING AN ASSHOLE

Although it may not be pleasant, letting someone go should be respectful, while still done in a firm and, most importantly, timely manner. There is more to this than simply offering a severance package. When letting a team member go, be sure to keep the following in mind.

DON'T DRAG IT OUT

Your gut rarely lies. I've made the mistake of dragging out letting a staff member go in the hope that they would improve with guidance and feedback. They didn't. All along, I knew they weren't right for the job and they would do far better somewhere else. Don't make that mistake; it is unfair to both you and them. As soon as you realize they aren't the right fit, let them go. They should get one chance to redeem themselves, but then let them go. They will thank you in the long run when they get a new job where their particular skillset allows them to excel.

GIVE THEM TIME TO FIND SOMETHING ELSE

Don't be a stickler for the rules here. If your company policy is two weeks but the person has a family depending on their salary, give them adequate time to find something new, even if it costs you a couple of extra weeks on the payroll.

OFFER TO HELP FIND THEM A NEW JOB

Perhaps you need to shrink the overall number of staff to keep the agency afloat and you need to let a loyal staff member go. Offer to help them find a new job by opening up your network and introducing them to contacts who might be able to employ them.

OFFER THEM A GREAT REFERENCE

Unless they stole from your company, or broke a client NDA, or really have murdered the office dog, and assuming they've worked with you for a while, always offer your staff a reference.

THE AFTERMATH

Remember, people leaving or being fired is traumatic for the team. Anyone who has worked at a medium- to large-size agency has no doubt experienced what I call the "Moses Effect": One or two departures leads to a mass exodus of staff. As such, departures on both sides need to be handled sensitively and carefully regardless of the situation.

WHEN NOT BEING AN ASSHOLE MAKES YOU AN ASSHOLE

A creative team requires clear leadership; no good shop is run by a democracy. The key ingredient to successful creative business is very simple: Produce fucking excellent work. It is more important than being popular. It is more important than keeping a disgruntled staff member happy.

From time to time, to succeed at producing great work, you will need to be an asshole. If you are not capable of being an asshole when needed, the work will suffer, you will lose clients and money, and you will eventually have to let staff go. Then you will be a *real* asshole.

To attract top talent you need to create an environment where people feel they can do the very best work of their careers. This means some level of healthy competition where individuals both drive each other and learn from each other. Young creatives learn more from their peers than from any senior management or classroom; when you have the best people, not only do they produce great work, but the learning effect multiplies the overall quality of the agency.

Being an asshole at the right times will be critical to your success. When we had outgrown our startup Santa Monica office at Edenspiekermann, my business partner and I had to choose between a cool downtown LA space or staying put on the Westside. A move to downtown would add a significant amount of commuting time for almost all our staff who lived on the Westside of LA. However, as the agency was expanding rapidly, we knew

THE DECISION SIMPLIFIER

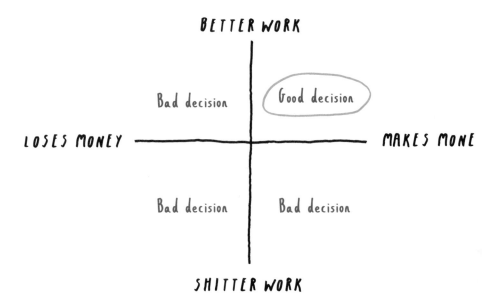

BETTER WORK

Bad decision   Good decision

LOSES MONEY   MAKES MONE

Bad decision   Bad decision

SHITTER WORK

that, for the growth of the business and for brand positioning (downtown was rapidly becoming the hub of creative business), downtown was the best choice, despite its unpopularity in the team. Everyone hated the decision, and probably us, at the time. There were complaints galore and we had to coerce staff in every conceivable way to keep them on-board. After a single week at the new space, every single staff member agreed it was the best decision we had ever made. Sometimes you just need to be an asshole and do what's best for the work.

Here are the most important things to know about when you *need* to be an asshole in order to make the best work in the business.

BE A CONTROL FREAK ...

While working at Edenspiekermann, we built an environment wherein the teams had full autonomy and decision-making power. However, I still made it a point to know the details of every major piece of work going out the door. There are two reasons for this. First and foremost, you need to know what goes on in your projects and ensure that the work is innovative and of the highest standard. To be a successful leader to your creative team, you need to know everything that goes on. Which client needs extra attention? Which client can be handled by mostly junior staff with oversight, and which client needs senior people for every interaction? Secondly, you need to be visible to your staff. In my experience, the hands-on creative director who gets his or her hands dirty and interacts with staff on a daily basis is far more effective than the recluse who hides in their office and delegates every task. These people are easily forgotten and never last long.

... BUT DON'T MICROMANAGE

You hired great people for a reason. Let them do their fucking job. They are probably more talented than you. Challenge them. Push them. But don't second-guess them.

PUSH CREATIVES UNTIL THEY ABSOLUTELY HATE YOU

There is no magic to creating great creative work, just hard work. It's a very simple formula: Iterate, iterate, and iterate some more. There is no shortcut. As an art director, design director, or creative director, it is your responsibility to push, push, push, and then push some more. Every creative wants to do great work, and if you're the idiot who doesn't push them to do that, you will be the *real* asshole if they have nothing worthwhile in their portfolio after years of working with you.

PEOPLE WORK BEST UNDER PRESSURE

There is a big difference between sustainable work (good) and lackadaisical attitudes (bad). Creatives should be able to work normal days, but they should work hard and fast when they are in the office. Creatives are more focused and work best when under pressure. If there is no deadline in sight, nothing will get done. When working in New York, we were under pressure all the time. It never fails to impress me how a tight timeline and a little bit of heat can drive a creative or a team to produce excellent work.

DESIGN IS NOT A DEMOCRACY

Every task, no matter how big or small, needs one owner and vision. The idea of a democratic leadership is bullshit. One leader, one big picture. Opinions are welcome, but decisions are not made by committee.

IF PEOPLE AREN'T GOOD ENOUGH, LET THEM GO

It's an unpleasant truth, but some hard-working creatives just don't have the skill to produce great work, no matter how hard they try. They often find their way into great agencies through portfolios that include big team projects in which they played a small role. Learn to spot individuals like this—they will need to be moved to an alternative role or let go. In my experience, sometimes creatives who lack the flair to do hands-on work can still play an important role in an agency. Many make excellent researchers or content strategists as they have a deep knowledge of design, even if they can't execute the actual design themselves.

BRUTAL HONESTY IS A BITTER, BUT NECESSARY, PILL TO SWALLOW

I had the great fortune of working for almost five years in Berlin and, unsurprisingly, with a lot of Germans. What I admire most about Germans (and Northern Europeans in general) is their no-bullshit attitude. If something sucks, they will tell you right away. They are honest (often brutally so) and don't sugarcoat things like Americans or Brits. While this directness can come across initially as harsh (I've seen many of our American staff almost in tears after a critical conversation with a German CEO), this openness means that people always know where they stand. Don't waste time with bullshit. Be direct and honest, even if it's not what people want to hear at the time. We can all agree the world would be a better place if there was less bullshit around.

GOOD DECISIONS	BAD DECISIONS
POPULAR IN THE LONG TERM	POPULAR IN THE SHORT TERM
MAKE MONEY	LOSE MONEY
MAKE BETTER WORK	MAKE SHITTER WORK
ARE MADE OBJECTIVELY	HAVE A PERSONAL BIAS
FOLLOW YOUR GUT	FOLLOW WHAT OTHERS SAY YOU "SHOULD" DO
ARE MADE QUICKLY	HAPPEN WHEN YOU DRAG YOUR HEELS

DON'T BE AFRAID TO THROW WORK AWAY AND START AGAIN

One of the toughest (and most unpopular) things to ask a team to do on a project they've been working on for some time is to start again. Unfortunately, sometimes this is what's necessary to produce great work. It does nobody any favors to try to fix a mediocre solution, even if they've been working on it for weeks.

A few years ago, I was working with a team on a big campaign that would go live in Times Square. After almost two weeks, the team had produced what felt like nearly 50 versions of the creative. While all were pretty good, none were really great or award-winning. It was the day before the client deadline, everyone was pretty exhausted, and we were about to start prepping the "best of a bad lot" for the presentation the next day. The creative director came in at 6pm, looked at the work, and tore everything down. We could have killed him. But sure enough, at 11pm that night,

THINK THE WORK ISN'T GOOD ENOUGH? TEAR IT DOWN AND START AGAIN. IT WILL BE WORTH IT.

we hit on the solution. It was a bold decision to tear everything down, but it was the right one. The bottom line: Think the work isn't good enough? Tear it down and start again. It will be worth it.

THE NON-ASSHOLE
MANIFESTO

THE NON-ASSHOLE MANIFESTO

1. I will leave my ego at home.
2. I will be direct, respectful, and honest with my team and my clients.
3. I will give credit where credit is due.
4. I will let people do their fucking jobs and not micromanage them.
5. I will cancel meetings that waste time.
6. I will write a proper briefing for every project.
7. I will give clear and constructive feedback.
8. I will let my team present their own work.
9. I will do everything I can to ensure no one has to work late nights or weekends.
10. I will reply to all job applications.
11. I will be fair and respectful when I have to let someone go.
12. I will strive for a diverse and inclusive culture in my workplace.
13. I will pay my fucking interns.

CUT OUT AND HANG IN YOUR SPACE

ACKNOWLEDGMENTS

This book started out as an idea after a heated argument with a friend about the necessity of working long hours in the creative industries. After I left Berlin for New York in 2015, I mused over the themes and ideas for almost two years before finally sitting down to write it in a remote cabin on Big Bear Lake in March 2017. The ideas contained in these pages are certainly not groundbreaking, or even original—they are simply a collection of common-sense morsels.

Much of the thinking in this book was inspired by my time working together with Erik Spiekermann in Berlin. I was lucky enough to work with Erik for several years at Edenspiekermann, starting out as an intern and eventually working my way up to Chief Creative Officer of the company. His no-bullshit attitude and the importance he placed on having a non-asshole culture has stuck with me throughout my career, and for that I'll always be grateful.

Finally, and most importantly, this book would not have been possible without my long-suffering wife Nora, who has been the driving force throughout my whole career. It was Nora who gave me the push to take a series of incoherent thoughts and ramblings and put them into the (semi) coherent format that you, dear reader, have just finished reading.

ABOUT THE AUTHOR

Paul Woods is an award-winning designer, writer and illustrator based in Los Angeles. He leads Edenspiekermann's creative and technology teams as CCO, building products, brands, and service design work for clients in industries as diverse as editorial, finance, sustainability, and transportation.

During his 15 years as a designer, Paul has been at the helm of projects for companies such as Red Bull, Google, Morgan Stanley, and Time Inc., among many others. An advocate for the power of user-centric design, Paul places a hyper-focus on the end user in his work. A thought leader in the design and technology spaces, his bylines regularly appear in publications such as *Fast Company*, *AdWeek* and *Communication Arts*.

In his spare time, Paul is an illustrator and co-founder of the satirical industry website Adloids. He lives in Pasadena with his wife Nora and a very stubborn basset hound.

He hates text that is written in the third person.

www.paulthedesigner.ie